B. WAYNE HOPPER
CLAUDE D. HOPPER

A Continuation of

HOW TO KEEP A CROWD

LISTENING

&

LAUGHING

A FEW SUGGESTIONS ALONG WITH A FEW STORIES, ANECDOTES, AND
AMIABLE OBSERVATIONS CONVENIENTLY COMPILED TO ASSIST THE READER
IN BECOMING A BETTER COMMUNICATOR.
PLUS BRAND NEW MATERIAL FROM CLAUDE HOPPER!

First Printing 1988
Second Printing Revised - March 2008
Third Printing Revised - November 2011
Fourth Printing Revised - September 2016
Copyright © by Hopper Brothers and Connie Publishing Co.
2811 US Hwy. 220 • Madison, NC 27025
www.thehoppers.com
Phone: (336) 548-2968

Proceeds from this book will go to Hopper Heritage Foundation - Madison, NC

Executive Fourth Printing Additions, Revisions, & Historical Research - Karlye Hopper
Associate Additions & Revisions. Executive Design & Graphics - Lucretia Kittinger
Cover photos and others contributed by ©DeDe Hopper - Used by Permission
Preliminary Story Board - Trevor Conkle
Video Production - Mike Hopper

ISBN 978-0-9831099-2-1

Printed by
EDMONDS PRINTING/COLOR IMAGES, INC.
Printed in the United States of America

*This book is dedicated to the millions of people who love
to laugh, and to the rest that so desperately need to.*

"A merry heart doeth good like a medicine..."
— Proverbs 17:22

Forward: A Brief Explanation

Growing up in a family of eleven children, especially in earlier times when culture was still somewhat primitive, brothers Claude and Wayne Hopper share their lives of day to day *survival.* They laugh, pretend to cry and often interrupt one another, vying to get to the punchline first. You may have grown up in a similar era or family situation as they and, if so, here's hoping you enjoy and can relate to this brotherly banter. If not, well, the pair hope you are at the very least entertained.

– Karlye J. Hopper

*All proceeds from *How to Keep a Crowd Listening & Laughing* benefit the Hopper Heritage Foundation, a non-profit organization awarding scholarships to budding youth in the fields of Christian music, studies and business & economics. To learn more about this great mission or to simply make a donation, visit hopperheritagefoundation.org.

A special thanks to the quoted men and women whose clever and novel statements helped to inspire and incite this brotherly collaboration:

ART BUCHWALL

BOTKIN

BENNETT CERF

THE DARTNELL CORPORATION

CHARLES GIBONEY

MEL GODFREY

BOB HOPE

CHARLES JONES

JIM MOODY

GENE PERRET

WILL ROGERS

ROBERT SHULLER

ZIG ZIGLAR

OUR FRIENDS & FAMILY

Table of Contents

Section I

Section II

CLAUDE HOPPER

Claude Hopper: I Blew Out the Lamp

Two of the greatest people I've ever known, besides Connie of course, happened to be my parents, James Archer (J.A.) and Dossie Pyrtle Hopper. Momma and Daddy met square dancing and Daddy always said that Momma was the best dancer on the floor. Daddy knew from the moment he saw her dance that he was going to marry her. When they first began courting, J.A. would come to the Pyrtle farm to water the mules and Dossie would make sure to have a note waiting for him under their rock. Before he'd leave, he would tuck her words in the pocket sewn next to his heart then quickly scribble down something he thought she would find sweet on whatever tattered piece of cloth he could find. When Daddy was sure no one was around, he would hide it back beneath that same rock. They would later marry (her, around the age of 16, and he a full decade her senior) and start a family. I'm pretty sure that when God said "go and replenish the earth," they thought they had to do it all by themselves 'cause that family would eventually include eleven children: Virginia, Monroe, Octola, Catherine, Paul, Will, Claude, Wayne, Steve, Richard and Dewey. Doctor Carter would ride in from town on his old mule to deliver each of us— these days, you go to *them*, where they park their Lexues, BMWs and Cadillacs!

I'm sure if you would've asked my parents about the best days of their lives, they would've been quick to mention the day of my birth - October 8th, 1937 (or so I was always told... We'll get to that later). I was born in a log cabin with no electricity (I was the only boy on the farm that played a kerosene guitar), in the backwoods of Madison, North Carolina on October 8th, *supposedly*. However, later on in life, as I went to apply for a passport I found out that according to legal documents, I was born on October 9th, 1937. After this, I went to my oldest sister who had both the family Bible as well as her own record, and both of those gave me two different birthdates! Since then, I have decided to celebrate the entire second week of October. You know, in case they still might have it wrong by a day or two—at least I'd get it right somewhere along the way. Being laughed at as a child and even into adulthood, I'm often asked why my mother would give a child such a name as Claude Hopper. Truth is, Momma didn't even get the chance to name me. Right after I was born, Momma fell into an unconscious state and couldn't tell you her own name, much less think up mine. The doctor looked at my daddy and said, "I've got to have a name for your son, Mr. Hopper." My dad looked over at the doctor kinda sideways and said, "Ah just call him Claude Hopper." Despite the silent war that would eventually wage between my parents, my dad held the kerosene lamp for my delivery. When I came out, they say I was so ugly I blew out the lamp and the doctor slapped my daddy!

My earliest memories are those from around the kitchen table where I can remember seeing a never ending circle of faces, devouring some of Momma's cookin', (which usually consisted of *at least* 40 homemade biscuits). We would all sit around a large table that Daddy built, I on one end and he at the other with everyone else squeezed onto benches on either side. All of our mugs and china were salvaged--just used army surplus. Even our blankets had been used during the war! As far as sleeping was concerned, you very seldom got chilly, especially since all eight of us brothers slept in one big straw-tick bed each night. The three sisters slept across the hall in the other room--that was all chocolates and roses--they had it made. Momma and Daddy slept downstairs with the newest baby at the time cradled gently into an antique crib. Well, by "antique crib," I more-so mean a Civil War era trough.

The family's means came by way of sharecropping, (and maybe later some moon-shinin', I never knew what all my crazy brothers got into). My grandmother owned the land on which we lived and tended a cash crop of tobacco. In order to feed the slew of us, our parents also grew a small vegetable garden; when we'd get through picking what we would need, (assuming it didn't look like a bunch'a wild hogs had just fled a crime scene), Daddy would take the leftover vegetables as well as the berries we had picked into town and barter at Meador grocery.

The Tallest in His Class

For seven years I attended school at Intelligence, better known now as Bald Hill. This was back in the day, when school lunches were less than a dime, and in order to catch the bus you had to walk a mile up a muddy road*. Each morning before school, (at about eight or nine years of age), it was a responsibility of mine to milk at least three cows before leaving. Momma taught me all about it since Daddy didn't know the first thing about milk cows—this became my very first job on the farm.

When I was in the third grade, I ran straight home and couldn't wait to tell my mom that I had the biggest foot in my class! I was very curious to see if it had anything to do with my Scots-Irish background. She looked at me with pity for a wounded puppy, "No, son, it's because you're 17 years old!"

In the fifth grade, the teacher looked at me with pride,
"Claude, you passed! You can proceed to the sixth grade!"
Shaking my head and staring straight at my feet,
I mumbled, "I'm not going."
"Well, you've graduated from the fifth grade, now it's time you move on to the sixth."
"I'm not going," I said again, this time with more fervor in my voice.
"Well just why not, Mr. Hopper?"
Trembling, I cried, "My daddy's in there!"

I must admit, however, that in the fifth grade, the teacher and I were the two most popular people in the class—we were the only ones with our drivers licenses.

Now later on in our small county, if you were sixteen years old and had a license, they would train you to drive the school buses. I'd drive a bus, pick up the kids and then siphon the gas out of the bus to put in our cars. However, often times on the way to school the bus would run out of gas. Eventually the superintendent caught on to my master plan and said, "Hopper, if you don't mind, could you at least leave us enough gas to get to school?"

*(The road I refer to here, where Connie and I still live today, was called 'Hopper Road' for most of my life. It was eventually changed when the State came in to put our little lane on a state-wide map! However, the day the officials came by to permanently title the long dirt stretch, all of us were out of town singing; instead, today, there is a different family name affixed to that road sign...)

The Hopper Brothers & Connie

ON THEIR WAY

"I'm Bound for That City"

My momma used to make us walk to church every Sunday, even for Bible school. We started out having to make the entire trip on foot, *both* ways, but eventually a neighbor, (note: our closest neighbor lived three miles off the main highway), was kind enough to drop us off at the end of our road. As a young boy, I can remember my family gathering to sing around the kitchen table. Momma was very musically inclined and always encouraged us to sing. She could play the harp, the piano and hum like a bird. Just before I turned 12 years old, I bought my first Silvertone guitar with the money Momma kept in a special bank for me, (I paid a whopping $7 for that hollow six-string). If I only knew how to play... While listening to WCKY, I heard Wayne Raney and Lonnie Gosslin advertise a guitar book with clever tips and tricks to teach beginners the basic chords of the guitar. Ah-ha! Boy, was I great... Ask any of my brothers!

The Lord came into my life when I was a young teenager, and I firmly believe that can largely be attributed to my momma and her adamance that we attend church. More than that, were it not for her love and prayers during that tender time in a child's life, I might not have been interested in attending the concert that changed my life... forever.

One of the most influential moments that would lead to our singing career came in 1956. I was around 19 at the time and had heard on the radio about this concert that would be held at Reynolds Auditorium. This was an annual singing that took place every Friday after Thanksgiving, the only difference this year was that *I was going to be there*. Boy, I'm sure glad I did! My world was flipped upside down, and in the best way possible! This particular concert consisted of the Statesmen, Blackwood Brothers and the Speer Family. I recall as Dad Speer began to walk the stage, rubbing his hands through his white hair, and started singing "I'm Bound for That City." I began to weep. The way he was singing it, I thought he was going to That City that night and I *wanted to go with him*! I'm a conservative baptist but this made me shout! I had brought another girl with me that evening and I haven't seen her since (this was before Connie and I were dating, of course). I came home that night knowing the desires of my heart—I wanted to be a part of this life-changing music. The next step was to drag four dusty farm hands out of a field and onto a platform, thankfully, if God be for you who can really be against you?

Shortly after this concert, in 1957, the brothers and I started singing with the accompaniment of my $7 Silvertone. We started out playing local church homecomings and revivals (often, more than one a day); but, soon, began attending every singing convention there was in the state. The more opportunities we had to sing, the more we looked to Dr. Peterson for voice lessons. One day during one of my lessons he turned to me and said, "Hopper, you've got a funny voice." Crushed, I asked, "What do you mean I have a funny voice? I'm trying to make a living with this voice." He said, "You have a prisoners voice. It's always behind a few bars looking for a key."

One of the greatest teachers of voice to ever grace the Gospel music realm was Leroy Abernathy. He could play "Jacobs Ladder" forwards and backwards while jumping on a pogo stick; he also had a two man quartet with Shorty Bradford where the duo could sing all four parts. One of the most profound things I've ever heard came from Leroy's lips, "Claude," he urged, "remember, singing is almost entirely attitude. It's a mere 10 percent talent and 90 percent attitude." As years have gone by, I continuously try to remind myself of this. I can recall folks approaching me on my so-called success, to which I can only reply with, "If I've been successful, it is only because you have made me that way."

A few have asked me if I knew Connie before she began playing piano for The Hopper Brothers. Well, I knew of Connie from high school but I didn't actually get to know her until spending time with her when the quartet would rehearse. She was two grades behind me and I remember that she would always play the piano during the assembly programs at school. I also knew that she sang and played the keyboard for a pop group, (think Fats Domino, Chubby Checker and Jerry Lee Lewis), and they were about to head to the Big Apple to "make it big"... Coming from a talented family, I knew whatever musical path she chose to follow she would easily succeed in. Clearly, I would have to act quick if I was going to convince her to play the piano for a bunch of country boys. In fact, I felt I needed to act so quickly, that one day while I was delivering groceries for the A&P, Connie pulled up at the stoplight and I ran over to knock on her window. Startled, she rolled it down. I didn't say a hello or a howya doin', I got straight to the point, "My brothers and I have started a quartet and wonder if you would be interested in playing the piano for us?" She told me she would have to take some time to really think about... Well, the light turned green, and she said yes!

Connie was always known for her unique voice and is by far the best thing that ever happened to the Hopper Brothers. In 1964, we attended our very first National Quartet Convention—and this trip would prove to be the beginning of a long list of first time experiences for us. It was our first time at NQC both as individuals and as a group, we all took our first flights to get to Memphis, and we were entering our very first talent competition. Even more, we ended up placing first—thanks to God and Connie—out of the eighty-two groups who entered and performed. The group must have taken it as a sign 'cause in 1965, we bought our first bus—a beat up 1948 Greyhound 3751 that we spent our life savings on... around $5,000. She was a beauty. Trying to manage the group while holding down a "regular" job was no easy task. Some days I'd step directly off the bus from singing all weekend, jump in my truck and head straight to work. The stress from it all is thought to have been the cause of me developing Bells Palsy at a young 25 years of age. I thank the good Lord for His healing hand during that challenging time and situation.

Our first bus

Claude & Connie Hopper

WHEN IT FIRST CAME TOGETHER

The Hopper Brothers & Connie

A GIANT LEAP

If I Can Help Somebody

My prayer is to be remembered as one that uplifts and encourages. More importantly, I want to persistently walk in such a way that as paths cross with my fellow man, they will feel supported and even advanced—not by me, but by the Christ that lives within me. Now, I don't mean the type who is so encouraging, he ends up encouraging another to jump right off that bridge... But you know what I'm saying. As the old cliché goes, "If you ever see a turtle sitting on a fence post, you know he did not get there by himself." I was, and continue to be, that turtle—if I have ever succeeded at something, it has been because of someone else's investment into me. Naturally, this is what prompts my prayer to pass this along. Further, please allow me to urge you, never give up in life... God had a plan for a life even like mine, and He has a plan for yours. Throughout my decades, I've faced Bells Palsy, multiple strokes, cancerous polyps, even a TIA or two. I'll never forget after my last stroke, when I was in the chopper being transported to a bigger and more equipt university hospital, I told God that I was ready to go. *I meant it*, too, but the humanity within me also asked—if He saw fit—to leave me on earth for a little while longer... I told the Lord how much I still wanted to accomplish and that, if He would spare me, I would only do those things one way—with Him. I felt like Hezekiah as he became ill, turned his face to the wall and cried out to the Father in II Kings. A few weeks later, at a Baymont Inn in Madisonville, Kentucky (not far from where I was when the stroke had occurred), God spoke to me. It wasn't an audible voice, nor did He use any magnificent light from above. In a way that I will never be able to explain, I heard, "I'm going to give you those years, now let's do this together." Through all things, God has been faithful and I give Him nothing but praise and glory.

...Some Not-So-Final Thoughts...

One of my favorite quotes came from the mouth of a man by the name of Will Rogers. Real simply, he stated, "I never met a man I didn't like." This is such a profound and simple truth. "I've never met a man I didn't like; I've never met a man I couldn't learn from." In fact, every person I've ever met was an opportunity... Think about it... Everyone you encounter on life's journey has taught you something. Whether it's something you should be doing or something to definitely avoid, you've learned something.

The Hoppers

THE MISSION IN FULL BLOOM

As you all know them
today, cutting up
at a recent photo shoot.

- For our fifty-fourth wedding anniversary, I took Connie to Honolulu, Hawaii, for some much deserved relaxation in paradise. Truthfully, I've always loved it over there for the history... The Punchbowl cemetery where we laid to rest innumerable American veterans, not to mention Pearl Harbor and the USS Arizona where there are still thousands of men and women entombed—it's a very special and emotional place. Now I know that as we get older, we become slightly lesser versions of our once-superhero selves. As I was coming off the gangplank of the Arizona, I spotted a man I hadn't seen in fifty years. Grabbing my arm, he said, "Was it you or your brother that got killed in World War II?" I said it was me. He replied, "I thought so."

- I went to Wal-Mart the other day—our town just got one, Connie had been shopping at the A&P grocer (that now doubles as a Pizza Hut) since we met—and met a blind man who had a seeing-eye dog. Everyone around saw 'em pick up that dog and swirl it around and 'round in the air by the leash. My own curiosity got the best of me, so I asked, "Sir, can I help you with something?" Turning towards my voice, he said, "Oh, no, I'm just looking around!"

- I talked to a friend the other day whose wife had just started drinking Slim Fast—he said things were going great and she was losing an average of ten pounds a week! With excitement in his voice, he said, "Think about it, at this rate, she'll be gone in 18 weeks!"

- Connie and I had just gotten married and decided to go to the Grand Canyon for our honeymoon. We had gotten quite a ways into the thing, so I asked if she'd like to ride around the rim of the canyon to see the beautiful vegetation and Colorado river. When she said yes, I did the logical thing and rented us a set of mules. We headed out for our stroll but, after a short way, her mule stumbled and I could tell it frightened her. Now, I married a tough farm girl, so she carried on but I overheard her say to the mule, "That's one!" We got down the trail a little ways further and the mule stumbled again, but this time she lost her backpack and all her drinking water. Again, I heard a faint, "That's two!" Almost to the end of our ride, her mule bucked her slap off and she hit the ground. Connie got right up and, in the same tone she used to discipline our boys, said to the mule, "Now, that's three." She looked to me and asked if I had brought along my pistol. Before I could even answer she had it out of my hand and had shot that mule dead. I'd never seen anything like this, especially out of my new bride, so I got stern real quick, "Connie, we just got married, and I'm the man of this household. Do you understand me? Don't you ever let anything like this happen again." Connie cut her eyes at me, "That's one!"

- Some new statistics show that 68% of the entire male population is on some sort of medication... And the other 32% are walking around untreated.

- Just when I was getting used to yesterday, along came today.

- Age doesn't always bring wisdom. Sometimes age comes all by itself.

- God, please grant me the senility to forget the people I never liked, the good fortune to run into the ones I do, and the eyesight to tell the difference.

- Someday, I'll look back on all I've done and plow right into my favorite John Deere.

- The early bird gets the worm... Now that don't say much for the worm, does it?

- Like the old sayin' goes, "Never say anything about a man until you've walked a mile in his shoes" ... By then, he's a mile away, you've got his shoes, and you can say whatever you want to.

- Not long after Connie and I were married, I had to drive up to for Virginia for a meeting with my then-boss. My mother-in-law, Mary Lou Shelton, had never been out of our small town so we decided it would be nice to take her on this quick day trip. No more than five minutes down the road, Connie yells for me to speed up so we won't be late. Next thing I know, my mother-in-law screams, "Claude, if you don't slow down my hair is gonna fly right 'out this car!"

After two hours and twenty mixed signals, I looked at Connie, "Who's driving this car—you or your mother!?"

- A clear conscience is usually a sign of a bad memory.

- A recent study shows that 70% of the time, my wife is right all the time.

- As you grow older, do you miss the innocence and idealism of your youth, or do you mostly just miss cherry bombs?

- A middle-aged man was in church on Sunday morning to hear his well respected preacher deliver what would be one of his lengthier sermons. About halfway through, the man disappeared from the sanctuary until the dismissal prayer. After the service had ended, the preacher went running after this suspicious congregation member and insisted he know where he had wandered off to during his teaching of the Word. The man smiled, "Oh, I had to get a hair cut." Angered, the preacher raised his eyebrows and his voice, "Well, why didn't you get it before you came to church!?" "I didn't need it then," said the man.

- A little girl went to her mama and asked "Mama, where do we come from?" Her mother replied, "Well, God created Adam and Eve and they had children and their children had children and we're a part of all those children." Two days later, the same girl decided to ask her dad the same question, but his response was a little different. "You see, honey, a billion years ago, we evolved from apes, gorillas and monkeys!" Distraught, the little one went back to her mama, "Mama, Daddy says we evolved from apes, gorillas and monkeys?!?!!" Without batting an eye, her mother quickly stated, "I told you about my side of the family, and that's his side."

- Growing up, the most exciting thing we heard about (year-round) was the North Carolina State Fair that took place in Raleigh every fall. After eleven kids' worth of begging, Daddy finally agreed to take us! He loaded all of us, plus Momma, into his 1929 Model A pickup truck and headed off on the ninety mile journey to our state's capital. Once we got there, Daddy hopped out and went to the ticket booth alone, "Sir, me and my family drove ninety miles to come see the world champion bull you're showing here this year... Can I get a discount?" Confused, the teller came out of his booth to ask, "Why should I give you a discount?"

"Well," Daddy said, "I have a rather large family. You see, here are my eight boys and there are our three girls... My wife and I add up to thirteen."

"Go on in with your whole family for free, Mr. Hopper," said the teller, "I want the bull to see you!"

- My brother Wayne was very popular in college—in fact, he was elected President of his freshman class both years.

- I met a man in Tucson that didn't have no ears. I hollered real loud, "Sir, what happened to your ears?" He mouthed, "Well, I was ironing my clothes when the phone rang and I put the iron to my ear." Out of plain curiosity I had to ask, "Then what happened to the other one?" Finally, he hollered, "They called back!"

- One sister said to the other, "Why does Grandma read that Bible all the time?" The other said, "She's cramming for finals."

- I had just gotten engaged to Connie when I was drafted and required to report Fort Leonardwood. I couldn't wait to get back and see that beautiful brown-eyed lady. When I arrived home I went by my Dad—born in the 1800's, he was already an older man then—I said to him, "Dad, I've got half-a-mind to marry Connie." Without looking up from his morning paper he said, "Son, all you need is half a mind."

- I've never thought of myself as a genius...but my brothers can be just plain dumb. One day, Richard and Dewey met up on the riverbank to go swimmin' and noticed Steve across the water. The boys yelled out, "Hey, Steve, how'd you get on the other side?" Steve yelled back, "You're on the other side!"

- I recently went for a routine physical. After checking out my chart, the doctor looked at me sideways and said "you're fat." Offended, I insisted on a second a opinion. To which he replied, "Well you're ugly too!"

- With eight Hopper boys (those are just the ones from my dad's line—Daddy had brothers and cousins with sons who went to the same high school as all of us) constantly trying out for, being on, graduating from or getting kicked off of the football team, the Madison football coach really hated to see us coming. I wasn't a bad player. In fact, I was better than the rest of my brothers, but my last name kept me on the bench a lot of the time. However, there was finally a game where we were down a player and the team really needed me! Coach came over to the bench, "Hopper, can you pass a football?" Innocently, I said, "Gee, sir, I don't rightly know if I can swallow it."

- The last time I went fishin', I caught one so big that I couldn't get in the boat... So I took a picture of it. The picture weighed 27 pounds.

- Several years ago, Connie had taken some time off from the road to write and rest. When it came time for her to rejoin the group, I decided to take her out to dinner before leaving on the bus that night... The lights were dim when I handed her the letters she had received while she was away, so she slid on her glasses and began to glance through them. Looking over at my lovely wife, knowing what all we had been through together, I said, "Connie, I'm so very proud of you and all that you stand for." I continued talking and complimenting while she just kept reading them letters! Finally, I raised my voice, "Connie, I said I'm proud of you!"

Lowering her glasses she looked up at me and yelled, "Well, I'm tired of you, too!"

Claude & Connie Hopper

IN 2015,
CELEBRATING 58 YEARS
OF MUSIC MINISTRY.

Q & A with Claude

1.) When did you decide to insert humor into your work in Gospel music?

A. Too early and often. I wasn't very good at it, and that can't be taught or polished over, it sounds unauthentic. I can be a bit corny, but all generations can relate to that humor. I want them to see themselves and also realize Christians are allowed to have fun... There is far more meaning and joy when we do so, it's a praise to God... Proverbs tells us that humor and joy do as a medicine. The Bible says we were given a time to laugh—did you know that it is psychologically impossible to think negatively while laughing?—audiences connect when you insert humor.

3.) You were young when you accepted Christ, correct?

A. Quite young—right there at our old country church (Ellisboro Baptist), established in 1896 and still standing today. Then, in 1950, it was like an old school house fixed on cinder blocks with a potbelly stove for heat and kerosene lamps for lighting. Nowadays, it's one of the larger churches around, and growing by leaps and bounds. Just in the last year, Ellisboro has seen close to 100 salvations and just as many new members! It was my father's church, and his father's before him...and his father's before him. Come to think of it, the headstones in that church cemetery have only got about three last names.

4.) What's your take on the now-controversial subject of "formal education" costs?

A. The question is not can we afford the cost of education but, rather, can we afford the cost of ignorance? I was the first in my family to attend college and, at the time, the financial aspect of higher education was the very least of my worries. It wasn't long into my academic career before I was hit with the financial reality and, unfortunately, was unable to finish college because of it. This, along with being blessed to have met some of the brightest, most promising young people who simply weren't dealt an overflowing financial hand, led me to what I've now found to be my true calling. I saw a specific need, one I felt that I could make a small contribution to and really make a difference in, the need to aid people (young and old!) succeed and go farther in life. In 2003, our family began a public 501C3 foundation—The Hopper Heritage Foundation— that contributes to four college tuitions (per year) for qualified students. Our mission is to help young people pursue their passions and career in Christian music, business and economics. Presently, our funds are raised via a percentage of The Hopper's merchandise sales, donations and two golf tournaments, (one on either coast of the U.S.). All of these collective funds are matched by our partnered universities.

A Young Claude

FROM THE DAYS OF THE DRAFT

Claude & Connie Hopper

JUST-A-COURTIN'

Credit Where it's Due:

Books and Quotes Claude has read that may have contributed to the man he is today, they also may have been indirectly plagiarized in this work. This is an apology to those great authors in advance.

- Uell S. Andersen — *Three Magic Words: The Key to Power, Peace & Plenty,* 1954.
—*The Greatest Power in the Universe,* 1978.

- Claude Bristol — *The Magic of Believing,* 1948.

- Dale Carnegie — *How to Win Friends and Influence People,* 1936.

- Samuel A. Cypert —*Believe and Achieve: W. Clement Stone's 17 Principles of Success,* 1991.
- Cort R. Flint — *The Purpose of Love,* 1973.
"Love... The source of everything that is meaningful..."

- Napoleon Hill — *Think and Grow Rich,* 1937.
"Anything the mind of man can conceive and believe, he can achieve."
— *Succeed and Grow Rich Through Persuasion,* 1989

- Augustine "Og" Mandino — *The Greatest Salesman in the World,* 1968.
"Change your life with ten ancient scrolls... each scroll contains a principle which will drive a bad habit from my life..."

- Norman Vincent Peale — *The Power of Positive Thinking,* 1952.

- Proverbs 23:7 — "For as a man thinketh in his heart, so is he."

- W. Clement Stone — *The Success System that Never Fails,* 2004.

Wayne's Story: As Claude Remembers It

My brother Wayne was what you would call a problem child. We have a place down in North Carolina called Camp Butner, (which is where Madoff is today). Momma and Daddy sent Wayne down there to...well... "rehabilitate" him. The folks at Camp Butner worked and worked—before shock therapy was outlawed—until he was finally "cured," if you will. Upon his release from the facility, his counselors were so impressed with his improvement that they asked if he would take a bus load of patients out to a place called Meadow restaurant before he returned to Madison. My brother was so excited to be skipping Butner that he was more than happy to do this.

"I have a bus load of people being treated at Camp Butner," Wayne explained to the waitstaff, "you just need to know that they're gonna come up and pay for their meals in bottle caps that they've stolen from your store. Just take it like it's real money, and when they're all loaded up on the bus, I'll be back to settle up with you." Management agreed. Everyone finished eating and Wayne went back to settle the bill. Prepared for my brother to be the sane one, Wayne heard the total and said, "Do you have change for a hubcap?"

Well, when Wayne finally got to come home, the progress he made had regressed to the point that they had him sent to a place called Broughton, where they send the most severe mental patients. (The riskiest patients were placed on the third floor, behind bars.) One day, while looking through the bars over his window, he noticed several Broughton workers coming across the campus with a load of manure. Wayne hollered down, "Hey, what are y'all doin'?" They said, "We're cleaning out the stables. This manure is going to the field so we can put it on our strawberries." Wayne began laughing, hysterically, "Y'all are crazy! You ought to come up here—we put sugar on ours!"

Well, this might not all have been true, but it sure is funny. Now that you know everything about my brother, Wayne, it's time for him to defend himself..er..I mean, hear what he has to say...

SECTION II

WAYNE HOPPER

Who is Wayne Hopper?

In early spring of 1989, a wonderful thing happened to me . . . . I was diagnosed with cancer . . . surgery was recommended immediately with chemo to follow. . . . But let me back up a bit. . . my wonderful and loving wife Shirley had seen some tell-tale signs and ordered me to see a doctor. . . . this was no interest to me because I was on top of the world with my business life, tops in my company, my life was great. I was convinced that money, power and prestige were the most important items for me at that time. Little did I know that trying to lead an unholy life while trying to serve a holy God to no avail. . . it cannot be done. My many years of growing up in the church made me realize. . . . I was a backslider. . . I made the appointment with the doctor, he says we are operating in the morning after examining me. . . .you have cancer and we are going after it aggressively. . .my world came crashing down. . . it all came back to God and His angels and me!!!! I confessed my sins to Him and He restored me, I truly repented. . . . immediately I could feel the power of his forgiveness. He had never been that far away. . .He healed me of that cancer. . .the doctor called it a heralding episode. . . .I give God all the credit and glory for my healing and, for the people who feel the medical staff did the job, let me tell you that I feel He does work through them, but He is the Alpha and the Omega; nothing happens without His nod. . .let me tell you as a doctor told me, "We can treat, cut, saw, stitch and analyze, but God does the healing." I just thank Him each day and all the prayer partners across the country who came to my aid. . .prayer is the key. . .Now it is my hope you will draw from my experience to encourage others who may suffer at the hands of cancer. I continue to serve Him through my church and I have listened to the whisper of the Holy Spirit to entertain His people. Another wonderful story of equal importance is my wife, Shirley, and her experience. . . she was also diagnosed with cancer in September of 2006; after a few procedures and many prayers from our continued prayer partners and church family, one month, almost to the day, we are sitting in the doctor's office waiting for the pathologist report. . .he entered with a smile and says, "Mrs. Hopper, you are cancer free". . .we let out a little shout right there. However, in the winter of 2015, God saw fit to call my sweetheart home. He gave us several, wonderful, cancer-free years together but, please try to remember that God doesn't heal everybody. . .and if He doesn't, remember that He will sustain you. . . .there is a bigger plan for you, I am certain.

Sincerely,
Yours in Christ
B. Wayne Hopper

And the prayer of faith shall save the sick, and the Lord shall raise him up; and if he have committed sins, they shall be forgiven him.

Confess your faults one to another, and pray one for another, that ye may be healed. The effectual fervent prayer of a righteous man availeth much.

James 5:15-16

About the Author: By The Author

Some of the following information has been exaggerated, misplaced or perceived wrong; but, nevertheless, all possess truisms.

I was born to proud parents, James Archer Hopper and Dossie Pyrtle Hopper, on April 23, 1939, in Rockingham County, N.C. I grew up a normal child under very abnormal circumstances... finished high school at Madison, N.C. and attended East Carolina College at Greenville, N.C. . . . Spent three years in the Army with a tour in Korea. . . . Have served in a couple of C.E.O. positions and have climbed the ladder in a couple of companies usually dealing with sales. . . . I am known as a pretty good motivator, a decent after-dinner speaker, a fair husband, a good father, an excellent provider; I do my fair share of community involvement. . . have a deep and abiding faith in God and have done less than my fair share of church activities. . . my kids have all grown up. . . had four of them in college at one time and a twelve year old at home at this writing. . . . I now live in Lynchburg, Virginia with what's left of my family. . . . I serve as president of my own corporation and my wife, Shirley, retired from the Department of Motor Vehicles. . . . We are still surviving, but thanks to you who read this book, we can chase away a few wolves. . . . I have been extremely blessed with healthy kids and wife, with no catastrophes and a lot of enjoyment in family education. I get into all of that in my next book. . . .

Okay, so that's pretty much it and it sounds dull, doesn't it???? So, what I have done in the following paragraphs is go a little deeper into "about the author" and try to give details of how I was really brought around to this writing. . . . I hope you enjoy it.

The home I was born in was near Madison, N.C. and on this particular spring morning the sun was shining thru the window; there was an air-of-excitement but, at the same time, a special calm about the room. I, Wayne, was born the eighth child and fifth boy of a family of what I perceived as abject poverty, that would eventually have eleven children--eight boys and three girls. I was born healthy with no complications. My mother gave birth to all eleven and one stillbirth in the same bed, the same room of the same house--that old house still stands today, thanks to broth-

Claude

er Claude. It was a house of poverty (what I thought), a tenant-farm family raising mostly tobacco as a cash crop and raising other crops for survival. We were so poor, the poor people talked about us. We looked up to people on Welfare. . . . When <u>our</u> "rich" uncle died, it was in the Will--We owed <u>him</u> $20.00. Somebody sent our "Family Portrait" to some starvation countries to make them feel better. . they sent <u>us</u> food!!!! My dad allowed no mirrors in the house. . .he didn't want us seeing ourselves starving to death. I've seen times so hard, the worm would pull the bird in the hole. . . .We watched "Rat Patrol" ten years before it even came on TV. Our bedrooms were so small, the rats were humpbacked. . . when you closed the door at night, the doorknob got into bed with you. . .you had to leave the room just to change your mind. . . .The worst beating I ever received was when I was caught turning in bed (wearing out the sheets).

I may be kidding here, but, on top of all this misery, my brothers were all suffering from "Hypoglycemia." I called it just plain <u>dumb</u>! I had to have <u>the</u> dumbest brothers in the world. Let me give you these examples and you judge for yourself: My oldest brother "Monroe" was being interviewed for a policeman's job there

Monroe

in Madison. Now this was hard to do because in your background you would have to have worked at the Mule-pen there in Madison. Well, they overlooked this because Monroe had plowed Mules for years. On the oral exam he was asked: "In the event of a hostile crowd, how would you disperse them?" Monroe answered: "Take up an offering!" I was taking a sack of

Paul

pigs over to the neighbors once and my brother Paul asked what I had in the sack and I said: "Pigs." He asked: "How many have you got in the sack?" and I said, "If you can guess, I'll give you both of them." He answered: "Five." Paul had a beautiful bird dog, he was a perfect pointer. Paul shot him! I asked him, "Why did you shoot him Paul?" He replied, "I threw him up three times and he didn't fly." My brother, "Will," and I went fishing one day and I

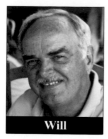
Will

was fortunate enough to land a biggie--I yelled to Will, "Mark this spot!" And Will pulled out his pocketknife and cut a mark in the side of the boat. I asked: "Will, what good will that do?" He looked up and said, "I see what you mean now, we may not get the same boat next time." I went with my brother, "Claude," up to a construction site when they were widening US 220 near our farm. We wanted to try and pick up a job. We approached the foreman and he agreed for us to go to work, he knew we were farmers and didn't mind work. He said for us to report that afternoon. Claude spoke up and said, "Just a minute, sir, what do you pay?" The foreman replied: "I'll pay you exactly what you're worth." Claude thought for a minute and said: "Doggoned if I'll work for that!!"

My next youngest brother, "Richard," and I went out for our first restaurant meal. He ordered steak and so did I. . . . The waitress asked him how he wanted it cooked, and he said, "Fried." She said, "What I mean is how long do you want it cooked?" Richard said, "About ten

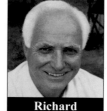
Richard

minutes." Well, when she brought the meal, Richard embarrassed the heck out of me... he picked the steak up with both hands and

Steve

started eating it like a chicken leg, with gravy dripping off his elbows. . . .It upset me so bad I dropped a whole handful of mashed potatoes.

Let me tell you a little about my brother, "Steve." He is the only "white" man I know that got a job as a porter on a train. He rode from Greensboro to Buffalo, New York and returned. On his first trip out a man came to him with a complaint--the man retorted, "Look at these shoes!" Steve asked: "What's the matter, aren't they shined good enough?" The man said, "You brought me one brown shoe and one black shoe." Steve remarked: "Doggone it, that's the second time that's happened this morning."

On another occasion a man approached Steve after leaving Greensboro and said to Steve that he needed some sleep, but definitely had to get off at Washington, D.C. and that it was very important that he do so. He went on to say that he was a sound sleeper and may put up a fight when trying to awaken him, but he said to pay no mind to his behavior and go ahead and get him off anyway. Steve said that he needn't worry about a thing. . .he would handle it. Well, the man woke up in Buffalo. . . and did he ever look Steve up and dressed him up one side and down the other. When the man had left, a bystander who had overheard this one-sided conversation couldn't resist putting in his two-cents worth. He said to Steve: "How could you take that kind of verbal abuse from that man in that manner, why, I would have had to hit him!" Steve replied: "What that man said to me was nothing compared to what that feller said that I put off down there at Washington, D.C."

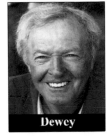
Dewey

"Dewey," my youngest brother, was probably the dumbest one. I visited him one day to find him skipping up and down the road. Naturally, I asked what a grown man like him was doing with such childish behavior. . .His reply was that he was following Doctor's orders and produced a prescription bottle with instructions that said: "Take two tablets, skip a day, take two more tablets. . . ." We were swimming and taking a few bets and dares down by Dan River one day. Well, all of us had swam the river and standing on the other side we began to yell to Dewey to come on over. . . .Well, Dewey swam to within three feet of the bank and turned and swam back to the other side. We yelled: "Why did you go back?" Dewey replied: "I saw I wasn't gonna make it so I came back." Dewey was summoned for Jury Duty. . . it happened to be a Murder Case. . . . The defendant's lawyer was picking the jury and came to Dewey, and asked: "Sir, do you believe in Capital Punishment?" Dewey replied: "Yes, if it ain't too severe!"

One of my sisters fell in love with a guy from Massachusetts. She finally broke the news to the family this way: "Daddy, what would you-all say if I told you I might marry a damn Yankee someday?" "Say," said Daddy, "I'd say we're finally beginning to pay them back at last."

Virginia

I had three sisters and they weren't as dumb as they were mean. So, you will notice that I don't mention their names. They also have husbands who average about the same as the line of the New York Giants and I'm not sure what they're capable of. One sister has been known to throw knives at us and another cut her own throat and crawled into the dog box to bleed to death. Still another started smoking when she was sixteen and would tell us she could make smoke come from her eyes. . . while we looked intently at her eyes she was burning us from the side. Are you now beginning to get my drift? (*My sisters hate this but it is just fun. . .*)

Toni

They were on the skinny side. One of them was so skinny - she had two backs, she held her girdle up with suspenders. She went to a carnival once and laid down on the "bed-of-nails" and fell thru. Another sister was skinny and bow-legged. We used to get her into a running race just to watch her run - it looked like an

Cathrine

eggbeater going down the road. If it hadn't been for her varicose veins she wouldn't have had any legs. When she would sit down her knees would make a fist. Another sister was given a "living bra" for Christmas one year - it died of starvation. She refused to wear striped pajamas because when she put them on you couldn't see but one stripe. She came home one night with rice in her hair and my folks said "Thank goodness you got married." She said, "No, a Chinese guy threw up on me." She swallowed a whole olive one time - scared us to death, we thought she was pregnant. All brothers and sisters became very successful in their ministry.

I cannot go further without mentioning my Dad. He's a great guy. Can you imagine trying to raise eleven kids? Eight of them boys? Wow! He was a considerate man though, every morning before breakfast he would teach us to swim. He'd put us in the boat, row us out to the middle of the pond and throw us over the side to make us swim to the bank. Of course it was a little difficult sometimes getting out of that sack and getting those trace chains untied etc. . . . (*just kidding*)

My dad was a stern man while we were growing up - never smiled, believed in the "iron hand" and "sun to sun" work ethic. He was a great fan of Christopher Columbus. He told us: "Now, here is a man that when he left home, he didn't know where he was going, and when he got there, he didn't know where he was, when he got back, he didn't know where he had been, and he did it all on somebody else's money."

He never bought us toys but, "hog killing" time was a "special" event for us. Not only did it give us fresh meat, but we were able to salvage that ole pig bladder, blow it up with a ragweed stem, tie off the valves, put it by the fireplace to dry, and behold--we had a football!! I'm here to tell you when we played with that thing-nobody ever fumbled it or was allowed to fall on it. Dad would take us to the County Fair each year but never bought us cotton candy or a candied apple or bought us tickets for rides--in fact he didn't spend any money that way. We were allowed to see all the agricultural exhibits, after all, agriculture was our livelihood. Everything else was tomfoolery.

Daddy got hooked on movies at one time and would frequent the local drive-in theater owned and operated by Pete Baker, a cousin of ours. Daddy always drove through and never stopped to pay.

On this particular night they had a movie with slapstick comedy and had a scene where three well-built women were undressing by a private lake and right before they'd be seen taking it all off, a train would come by, obstruct the view, and after the train went by the scene showed the young women in the water. Well, about 4 a.m. Peter was coming by from closing the concession stand and locking up when he spotted Daddy looking at this movie for the fourth time. Pete asked, "Hey Arch, are you gonna spend the night?" and Daddy says, "I'm gonna stay here till that train is at least two minutes late one time!"

Daddy is one of the few parents I know that would send you to cut your own switches to get whipped with and then inspect them for strength and durability. If they didn't pass the test you had to go get another. He allowed us no experience with luxuries. Our house had two bedrooms; one for eleven kids and one for Mama and Daddy. All eight boys slept in one big bed with a straw mattress, called a "tick" and I had a brother that tried to create the first waterbed forty years ago. Every year though, we got a fresh straw, and that was an exciting time in our lives. We'd shake all the old straw and bugs out of the old one and pack "new" in there.

Try to imagine sleeping with seven other people through your entire upbringing. Why, I never knew what it was to sleep alone until after I got married! Later on a friend of mine, with an airplane, and I took Daddy up in the plane because it was something Daddy had always wanted to do - to fly in an airplane. We flew him around the farm and the area - he seemed to be enjoying it tremendously. When we got back on the ground I asked him what he thought of the plane ride, he said, "Fine, but I never did put all my weight on the dad blamed thing."

Mama was a "Special" person - she was always there and quick with love and guidance. That woman could do so much with so little and did it for so long. She eventually could do anything with nothing. Mama could do more with four ounces of fatback than a New York chef could do with material for a three-course meal.

Mama cared for twelve people, that's right, twelve. Daddy got his share along with us. I remember her shaving him for years and turning his covers back and getting out his clothes and shining his shoes after we left home.

Washing was a whole-day job, "sun to sun" for her. My job was to build a fire under the pot for hot water. Mama got a day off from field work for "wash day." She got to leave the field 30 minutes early to go prepare lunch, or dinner as we called it. She usually got three days off to have a baby.

Plenty of time was spent caring for us - especially bathing us in that ole tub with a "2" on the bottom. I always thought that "2" meant for two kids. I would always get that same brother to bathe with, that did the number in bed. People are always asking, how did you know when he did it in the tub? That's easy - the water got warmer!!

Mama prepared three meals a day for us - and though they were skimpy meals centered around about 30 biscuits, we didn't know they were skimpy. What amazed me most was that she would start from scratch each morning and prepared those biscuits, along with the other meals, work in the field, care for the children and still have time to sew for us and other people, crochet, quilt, can and perform other household chores harder to handle than today because she had no running water or electricity for many long years. Most of us were in high school or had already moved away when running water and inside plumbing was put in.

When I would visit Mama, after moving away, and I would arrive at the old home place, there seemed a certain magic in the air. The wind blowing thru the pine trees there seemed so profound, the birds sang a certain way, the sun had a special brilliance to it and you could actually smell the freshness of Mama's flower garden and the apple trees. She was always there to greet you with that tremendous smile of hers. Even if her world was full of difficulties, you would never notice. She was SPECIAL! She would set all else aside and just be glad to see you. She never really had time for her world, it was already filled up with everybody else's world, but that's the way she wanted it and was happy for it. Now that she is gone, when I visit the old home place the magic is gone. It is said everybody leaves a void in people's lives when they die, but in Mama's case she left a void even in nature . . . . That wind through the trees can't even be heard now, the birds seem to be in a state of shock and are not singing, the flower gardens seemed to be in mourning and respond to no one else's care, even the sun doesn't seem to have the same brilliance. She was Special.

Mama made sure we went to Church and attended Vacation Bible School. She participated in all PTA meetings and kept a keen interest in our school work. She always encouraged our participation in good wholesome activities such as the 4-H clubs and made sure we had a good social life and that it was a well adjusted crowd.

When we got into high school, we found that the girls like athletes. So, we all went out for the major sports, all brothers anyway. We did this mainly for an image boost as I look at it today. Football was our first try-out and besides, we had experience with football when using that old pig bladder. Also, it was hard work and we were already used to that. Coach Raymond Cure called me over one day and wanted to know what position I could play-without hesitation I replied: "The End." He says "what makes you think so?" And I said: "Coach, that's what I have heard all my life, in fact the morning I was born my folks took one look at me and said 'That's the end'." Anyway, it didn't work that well. . . you see, I had a terrible complex-I only weighed 119 pounds and was 6 feet 1 inch tall. . . . That weight was with two bricks in my pockets. When I ran down the field with full uniform the pads slapped each other. . . .When I was tackled, it sounded like you had run into a pile of stove wood, and it usually hurt the guy tackling me because my bones cut him up pretty bad. . . I observed the other players laughing at me and overheard them saying: "If Hopper stood sideways and stuck out his tongue, he would look like a zipper." I was embarrassed to take a shower with the other players. . .number one, it knocked the breath out of me. . . .I had to jump around in it to get wet. . .I had to wear snowshoes to keep from being washed down the drain.

The Madison High Wildcats normally were in every game all the way up to the national anthem, but in my senior year we should have won the state championship. In that year, we had the best: our running backs could all run the 100 in ten seconds; our line averaged 218 pounds and were quick. With Hezzie Williams and Johnny Knight in there, it was awesome; our receivers could run down that field and execute the perfect patterns; we had great reserves; a great water boy in "Hootie Knight." We just had two minor problems - the quarterback stuttered and the center was goosey.

(I borrowed a few of these from other people from small towns.)

The town of Madison was a unique town in its own way. It was a typical "dull" town. Things were so dull there when I was growing up that we would go in to town on Saturday afternoons just to watch them give haircuts. My family wasn't from the town of Madison itself - we were from the suburbs called "Resume Speed." We had a "Miss Madison" Beauty Contest there for five consecutive years in a row. . . never had a winner!!! The town was so small, the telephone book had only one yellow page. The most excitement I ever saw was when the library caught on fire--burnt up both books. Our volunteer fire department was called and anybody could have put out the fire with two buckets in thirty minutes, but our fire department managed to keep it burning all night. The town was so small we had to take turns being the town drunk, and normally the town drunk had to play Santa Claus during the Christmas holidays. . .at least he was jolly.

In order to be a policeman in Madison you first had to graduate from the Livery Stable called the "mule-pen." One of our beloved cops, by the name of Walt, stopped a motorist and inquired as to where he was from. The motorist replied: "Baltimore." Our cop answered: "You're not fooling me, I know you're lying because I can see your 'Maryland' tags."

We had a community character (we had many community characters) whose name was Ira Paschal. Well, we never thought Ira had both oars in the water, but sufficed pretty well and always seemed to have money. Thinking this, two pretty good-sized fellows jumped him one day to rob him. Well, Ira put up the biggest fight you have ever seen a man put up. They finally subdued him and came up with 73¢. While lying there in the road, one of the thugs asked Ira why he had put up such a fight over 73¢. Ira replied: "Shucks, I thought you were after the $30.00 I had in my shoe."

We had plenty of folks that I hold dear back there in Madison--all cannot be named there--there was this particular African American family that we swapped work with and they lived and farmed on one of my Grandmother's farms. The name was "Brown." There was Walt, Frank, Booley, Lackey, and June. We would sit around during a rain storm or break and discuss world affairs and feel each other's head. We would remark that their head felt like lamb's wool and they said ours felt like a horse's mane. Walt Brown was the father and was a right old man. So, we asked him one day about what he thought contributed to his longevity--he thought for a minute and replied: "Well, when I work, I works easy; when I eats meat, I make sure all the fat's dried out, when I sits, I sits loose, and when I worry, I drops off to sleep." We were discussing accidents one day and I asked "Booley" what would be his choice if he could choose the accident he'd prefer to be in--if a "COLLISION" or an "EXPLOSION" were the choices. He answered: "A collision!" I asked, "Why?" He replied: "Well, when you are in a collision, there you is; but, when you are in an explosion, where is you?" I loved those people! We had a druggist there in Madison who could recommend anything for anybody. I heard him ask Pleas Godsey one day how the mud pack he sold him had helped his wife's appearance. Pleas replied mournfully that it did help for a couple of days, but then it began to fall off.

Madison had its share of doctors, but two of them were die-hards. Dr. Joyce was one of them. It has been told, that after examining a pretty young patient once, he remarked: "Mrs. Atherton, I've got good news for you." She interrupted: "Pardon me. Doctor, it's Miss Atherton." "Oh," said Dr. Joyce, "well in that case, Miss Atherton, I've got bad news for you."

Another doctor with "stickability" was Dr. Cox. It has been told that he wrote out a prescription in his usual legible fashion, like most doctors do, on such occasions to a tourist from up north. Well, the patient used that thing for two years as a "pass" on Amtrak: twice it got him into Radio City Music Hall; once into Ebbets Field. It came in handy as a letter from his employer to the cashier to increase his salary; and to cap it all off, his daughter played it on the piano and won a scholarship to the Curtis Music Conservatory. (*You have to know I stole that one*)

We had a banker there in Madison who believed in very little privacy. Should you need a loan and asked, he would repeat it to the entire back assemblage-$5,000 dollars!!! What in the world are you gonna do with $5,000 dollars???? On more than one occasion he would pretend to be hard-of-hearing. There was a spry old fellow that came into the bank one morning and sought a loan of $1,000 dollars. The banker yelled: "Speak up a little louder and reduce the amount a little."

There were two conventions going on at one time at Grogran's Motel there in Madison one year — one was a Used Auto Convention and the other was a Ministers Convention. By mistake, they served alcohol soaked watermelon to the ministers and by the time they discovered it, it was too late. Somebody asked what their reaction was, if any. "Well," said the waitress, "By the time I got in the room they had put all the watermelon seeds in their pockets."

We had a usual civil courtroom in Madison and if the case was too heavy, it was bound over to Leaksville for trial. We had trials of every sort. On one occasion an elderly woman, Maggie Vernon, obviously reluctant, was ordered to tell the court her eyewitness account of a fracas out in the country near her home. "Fact is, Jedge," she began resentfully, "it actually didn't amount to much. First thing I knowed Hal Carter called Bill Lineberry a liar and Bill knocked him down with a ax handle. One of Hal's friends got kinda riled and cut a slice outta ole Bill. Then Ed Jones, who was a friend of Bill's shot Hal, and two others shot him, and three or four more begin to get cut up a bit here and there. Well, Jedge, that nachelly caused a little excitement, and they commenced to fighting." (*Don't know where this came from but Hopper family don't like it.*)

We had our own hometown newspaper called the Madison Mess. It was a tremendous source of news and gossip and my favorite stories concerned two ads run there years ago. It seems an upstanding citizen who had attended a town meeting at the town hall was missing an umbrella. He ran the following ad to obtain its safe return; he also spent twice the cost of the thing on the ad itself; here it is: "Lost from town meeting last Friday: a black silk umbrella. The gentleman who took it will be handsomely rewarded by leaving it at number 14, Madison Post Office." It got no results whatsoever. A young copywriter there at the newspaper, David Spear, who happened to be the son of the editor, sniffed: "No wonder your ad produced no results, let me write one for you." It is as follows: "If the man who was seen taking an umbrella from the vestibule at Friday's town meeting does not wish to get into trouble and have an indelible stain cast upon his Christian character, which he values so highly, he will return it at once to number 14 Madison Post Office. He is well known!!!" The next day the man who lost the umbrella found five of them propped up at his box number at the Post Office. A local dentist, Dr. McAnnually, put this ad in the Messenger at one time. "Will the mother whose little boy laid his half-sucked lollipop on my mahogany end table come to my office at once--she can buy the end table with the lollipop still stuck to it."

Wonderful Memories are there in Madison for me and I sincerely hope nobody is offended by my humorous gestures in their regard, or on the town itself.

How to Keep A Crowd
Listening & Laughing

AUTHOR'S PREFACE:

Whether at a party, office function, conference, meeting, speech or seminar, and you are called on to contribute, you will need to keep that audience laughing in order to keep them listening.

Even if they are paid to listen, you will need to keep the lids to their minds open to receive your input. It can be done without "four letter" and "explicit" words.

ONCOMING LAUGHTER IS ESSENTIAL. . . .

My purpose in writing this book is to give you some important tips toward keeping that audience laughing and listening. It is not designed to make you a funny person - it is designed to give you tools to keep that person or people you are talking to listening.

After reading this report, you will not be an automatic comedian, or humorist or expert speech maker. However, what I will guarantee is that you will have all the tools and information necessary to make your contribution effective. But, like any other instructions, they must be followed. . . .

YOUR MATERIAL SHOULD SUIT YOU. . . .

In order to be successful, you must remember that "funny stuff" should be subjective. Each person has his own personality, thereby making you unique. Therefore, the material should be fitting to you first and foremost. Whatever that uniqueness is should be developed and nurtured.

The kind of "funny stuff" you do should be that which you like best and you feel most comfortable with. Please never try to be like somebody else - literally.

EVERYONE IS FUNNY. . . .

Some of you will probably say, I can't tell a joke. I can't be funny. I've never been able to make anyone laugh. I can't even remember jokes!

I'll bet if I could meet and talk to your wife, children, husband or close associates, I could prove you wrong.

LAUGHTER SUITS PEOPLE. . . .

Here is proof. . . . Last year in the United States alone, over 10 billion dollars (spelled with a "B") were spent for entertainment. Now let me ask you--what percentage of that sum was spent on laughter? or to entertain?

You get my point. The world needs humor more than it ever has in its history. Let us get in on the action of making it happen.

Many people have told me, "Wayne, you're better than Vegas." Now I'm not so naive as to believe that's true. I know they want to return some of the joy to me that I have given to them and are probably being kind. I know I am not that good; however, I am not so modest that I can't assure you that I can keep the crowd laughing and listening.

ORIGINALITY. . . .

Nothing you can say that is funny is original, nor can you tell an original joke. So don't worry too much about being original, novel, or first with the information or story.

I don't have to worry about original "funny stuff." I don't want you to worry either. The audience doesn't care whether it is "new" or not, as long as it is funny and they can relate to it. Also, I'm told by many that stealing someone else's material is not plagiarism but research--and sometimes just plain flattering.

Milton Berle's favorite comment was: "I know a good joke when I steal one."

Why Use Humor? AKA "Funny Stuff"

Naturally, I use humor in all my talks around the country. I find it enjoyable to me and especially enjoyable to my audiences. So, I ask all the time, "why not use humor?" It does the trick; it serves the purpose; it entertains; it's a change of pace for most meetings and conventions. The history of humor goes back. The Bible tells us according to Proverbs 17:22, "a merry heart doeth good like a medicine, but a broken spirit drieth the bones." Also, in Proverbs 14:30, it says, "a merry heart is the life of the flesh." In Ecclesiastes 30:22 It says, "Gladness prolongs his days." One of John F. Kennedys favorite quotes from the Bible was from Ecclesiastes that says, "There is a time to weep and a time to laugh. A time to mourn and a time to dance." It has been said that his administration appealed to many Americans largely because of Kennedy's capacity for fun. Bob Hope says that laughter is an instant vacation and that laughter and fun are the most wonderful tonics in the world. He should know; he has entertained G.I.'s all over the world and says he has seen the healing power of laughter. Of course, the more he makes people laugh, the more trips he can make to the bank. Henri de Mondeville, who lived from 1260 to 1320, was a great proponent of mirth as an aid to surgery. He was a great medieval professor of surgery. He would have friends and relatives visit the patient and tell him jokes to cheer him. His most famous quotation was, "The surgeon must forbid anger, hatred, and sadness in the patient and remind him that the body grows fat from joy and thin from sadness."

King Henry VIII kept a full-time jester by the name of Robert Armin. Queen Elizabeth I had Richard Tarlton as her jester. She claimed he could cure her melancholy better than all her physicians.

Robert Burton (1577-1650), an English parson and scholar, wrote Anatomy of Melancholy, one of the great books of Psychiatry. He could cite a large number of learned authorities in support of laughter as a therapeutic measure. The German philosopher, Immanuel Kant (1724-1804) believed that laughter is a psychosomatic phenomenon; certain mental ideas result in a bodily response - laughter - which has a beneficial physiological effect. You can find this in his book, *Critique of Judgment*. William McDougall, at one time a professor of psychology at Harvard, wrote an article proposing that the very biological function of laughter was one of helping to maintain psychological health and well being. Probably the most enthusiastic response to the role of laughter in health ever written is the book Laughter and Health, published in 1928 by the American physician, James J. Walsh. In his book it says, "There seems to be no doubt that hearty laughter stimulates practically all the large organs and makes them do their work better." Okay, I feel that I have made the point about laughter and that point has been backed up by some pretty authoritative people. There is one point I want to make at this time, and that is: The old conservative view of humor and humorists was that they were buffoons, crazy, idiots, . . . etc. Usually these were terms hung on "funny people," humorists, wits or comedians by people who were not. I know for a fact, and it can be substantiated, that you are loved "especially" should you be able to provoke laughter in another person. And, the more laughter you can provoke, the more you are loved. Essentially, you will find this to be true.

Stop for a moment and analyze the daily happenings -- you'll be hard pressed not to run into an effort of some type by someone who will try to invoke laughter or at least try to be humorous to get a point across or have people listen to them. You can start with the President of the U.S. and it comes down thru a number of TV sitcoms (which by the way are running at the top of the popularity chars) to the son or daughter, husband or wife, friend or relative on a daily basis who tries and usually succeeds in using humor or makes somebody laugh. Okay?

I think I've said enough about why use humor or "Funny Stuff." You have to realize it is very important and most essential in good communication.

God made man and woman and when you see me and look around at the rest - you must know He had a tremendous sense of humor.

Let's get on with the How's, When's and Where's . . . .

A couple of anecdotes for your pleasure. . .

"If you travel the straight and narrow, not many folks will try to pass you."

"A wife who has good common horse sense never becomes a nag."

"My mama said a woman had three (3) choices when meeting a domestic crisis. She can sue for divorce (never), have a good cry or rearrange the living room furniture."

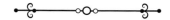

Wayne & Shirley

A HAPPY MARRIAGE OF SOOOO MANY
YEARS ALWAYS STARTED EACH
DAY WITH A LAUGH . . . .
SOMETIMES NOT . . . .

Daddy

WAS NOT HAPPY THAT I
LOST THE UGLY BABY CONTEST

NOTE: WE WERE A TWO CAR FAMILY;
2ND CAR IN THE BACKGROUND

I (WAYNE) ADMIT IT. . . I WAS A

Momma's Boy

ISN'T SHE BEAUTIFUL???

WE LOVED TO SEE

Uncle Irving

COME VISIT. HE ALWAYS HAD A STORY
AND A LAUGH (HIS FRIEND HAD
LAUGHED OUT). DON'T ASK
ME ABOUT THE SOCKS...

How Do I Get the Material for My Talks?

(Anything from Humorous to Funny Stuff)

Later on, I'm going to <u>give</u> you some material - first, I'm going to give you the "<u>Secret</u>" places to obtain all you'll ever need in the way of material that is funny, humorous or comical. Now don't be fearful that it has been heard before - good funny stories are never told too many times.

I've had people, that have introduced me at their particular club or function, say that they have heard me dozens of times and hope that I will tell the same stories they have heard many times before. However, I have several formats and don't tell the same stories each time and they are disappointed when I don't tell all of them. Speakers are not unlike singers when they have a hit song - you can have a hit joke - use it many times.

I know you like a particular comedian or personality or TV host and when he tells something funny or witty we are disappointed when everybody in our sphere of influence didn't hear it.

So don't worry about being novel or original - just wrap your own personality, and if possible, your family or background around it.

Okay, now for the "Secret" places you'll find material.

1.) LIBRARY - yes, that's right!! The Library. First you'll need a library card, should you not have one. People at my library know me by my first name - I frequent the place almost weekly.

Most libraries have subject "Humor" on their computer or "microfiche." Look up "Humor," "Humorous Stories," "Humorist," "Wits," "Anecdotes;" you'll find everything you need for a good talk or presentation. Pick out subject material that suits you, your personality and your audience. Also, remember to get material that will illustrate your communication or will help make the point, or like me, I just plain inject humor for a break in the presentation.

2.) NEWSPAPERS AND MAGAZINES - That's right, the newspapers and magazines are another "Secret" place. Are you beginning to get the idea. . . now that these so-called "Secret" references are already known?

Yes, in other words, I'm not giving you any secrets - I'm just reminding you of where they already are.

Newspapers and magazines are full of stories that can be

used. Most newspapers and magazines have a comic section. Most magazines have a joke section or have illustrations. Just take them all and place them in a reference file and when you have time, try and structure a story around them.

Let me give you an example of taking negative news and turning it into humor. . . . Headlines told of a man who came home to a stranger in the house and commenced to pursue and ultimately murder him. It unfolded as to several concepts but in follow-up pieces it revealed the murdered man had been having an affair with the wife of the gunman.

So, I made a short comment (humorously) in my next talk as an opener by saying - in the morning newspaper there were headlines that a man who had not kissed his wife in fifteen years shot another man for doing it. Well, needless to say, it was funny enough to bring down the house - but at the same time made a great point. "Kiss your wife more often." I followed up the opening remark, after laughter, by saying, "Need I say more?" Well, the women in the audience liked it especially.

3.) EVERYDAY LIFE - Yes, that's a great source of material - everyday happenings - asking all the people you talk to for a story. You will get a lot of material you cannot tell and a lot you already have listed, but nevertheless, you will get some for future reference.

There are certain individuals in the community that are always a good source of jokes and stories.

4.) TV & RADIO - One of my biggest sources of material is air media. I listen to all shows I can that can be helpful. I even listen to the "blue" comedians in hopes of picking up something that can be cleaned up for public consumption.

Evangelists, preachers, ministers and priests are also a good source of material. Just tune them in and you'll receive numerous stories.

5.) MYSELF & MY BOOK - Another source. I have them listed in chapters six and seven and you can come visit me at my next speaking engagement and get a few more. Professionally, I can't give them all to you.

More anecdotes . . .

" I knew a woman who had cooked so many TV dinners, she thinks she's in show business. "

" Face powder can catch a man but it generally takes baking powder to keep him. "

" I don't think the world is worse, it's just that the news coverage is better. "

"These new lipsticks in different flavors may be alright but there was nothing wrong with the good ole days when you kissed a girl and all you tasted was girl. "

"People at one time called me a "Bonanza Baptist. " I went to church on Sunday Morning but I stayed home on Sunday night to watch Bonanza. "

"When a girl starts calling you "sir, " about all you've got to look forward to is your social security. "

"For the single guy - This might help you in telling a woman's age. If she looks old, she is old. If she looks young, she is young. If she looks back, follow her. "

"The best way to remember your wife's birthday is to forget it once. "

"For the farmer and others - It's perfectly all right to pray for a good harvest but the good Lord expects you do keep on (hoeing) digging. "

When I Use My Material

Okay, you've now got tons of jokes, gags, anecdotes, and stories. When is the appropriate time to use them? Here's my answer - "Too soon and too often!!" In other words, start immediately. When I get material and it's new, I try it out on my wife, my kids, my secretary or anyone else that's close to me and can offer an objective opinion. I have to "bounce it off somebody" as soon as possible. Never try it on "John Q. Public." When he gets it, it's for real!!

You've got to put your material into four categories for proper use. Then when it's time to organize your delivery, you'll choose so many for (1) "openers," so many to (2) "illustrate points," so many to use as (3) "breakers," and "entertainment," and finally so many for (4) "closers."

Remember now - put the material into these categories.

1. Openers
2. Point Illustrators
3. Entertainment & Breakers
4. Closers

Now, I knew you'd get me to do it sooner or later. . .I'll demonstrate each category. . . .

1. OPENERS. . .

After being introduced by material I furnish the program director or toastmaster, I am now in front of the podium. I do not acknowledge the introduction at this point - I must come hard with an "Opener." Example - "Let me warn you that at my last speech, somewhere around three-fourths finished, I noticed there was only one person left in the audience. I remarked to him my appreciation for him staying - he said, "It's okay, I'm the next speaker." (Self deprecation is a must.)

"I've always wanted a little hand when introduced and that was little enough."

2. POINT ILLUSTRATORS. . . Here are two!

"We don't appreciate things so much anymore, we should always be positive in our appreciation. I know a little old lady that didn't have but two teeth. . .but she thanked God they met!" Another example: "Two soldiers are in the stockade - the first asked,

'How long you in for?' The second soldier replied 'Two years.' The first soldier asked - 'What'd you do?' The second soldier said, 'I went AWOL. And how long are you in for?' The first soldier said, 'Two days.' The other soldier asked, 'What'd you do? the first soldier said, 'Shot a General.' The second soldier said, 'What?? I go AWOL and get two years and you shoot a General and get only two days, how'd that happen?' The first soldier says - 'They hang me on Wednesday.' The point made was rather than looking at the extreme he only looked at the time in jail - you get it!!!

3. BREAKERS AND ENTERTAINMENT. . .

I have to tell you this - Joe Doe (furnish name) seated over here was alleged to have been - now that's what I've heard, I don't know for sure, it's just what I've heard, anyway, he was having trouble with his bull and called the vet in to examine him because it was breeding season and Joe wanted a good crop of calves. The vet left Joe some pills for the bull and Joe says that bull really went to town after he gave him the first dose. Somebody asked Joe - what kind of pills they were and Joe said he didn't know, but they were about the size of a quarter and tasted like peppermint!

Another example of "Breakers and Entertainment" . . .

Everybody knows that when Bill Smith over there has had one or two too many he takes his glasses off. I was talking to his wife of twenty years before I came on tonight. I said, "It must be easy for you to tell when Bill's been drinking anytime he comes home without his glasses on." She said, "What glasses?"

A "Breaker" is used to keep the audience from nodding or losing their concentration to what you're saying. Remember, the attention span of human beings is about thirty seconds at most. . . keep injecting humor "Breakers" whenever you feel they are needed.

Entertainment examples and Breakers are just pure jokes or funny stories that relate to nothing, make no particular points at all and are used in sequence when dealing with pure crowd pleasing. This is the closest you will come to being a comedian. You'll see Bob Hope doing this a lot or maybe Jackie Mason or Henny Youngman. Examples: "My family was so poor. . . we never had toys - I used to slide down the hill on my cousin, ---she wasn't too bad. . . we were sent to school with shoe polish on our feet and our toes laced. . . .we couldn't afford lunch money so we would take an eight pound lard bucket of milk and cake of corn bread - at lunch time we had a "crumble-in," we crumbled all that corn bread into the lard bucket of milk and we would sit around it with our own spoon and eat like pigs around a trough. . . we were so poor that our cash bounced. . . . the last time thieves broke into our house, they left something. One good thing about being poor, the doctor healed us fast.. . . Are you getting the idea?? Now you can't just say these one-liners and expect an automatic laugh. You may get a courteous laugh, but not serious laughter without first applying the inflections necessary to make them go over. Add to them some type of facial expression or gesture and the audience will come to life. Certain mannerisms applied to one-liners or pure-fun statements also can make an audience come alive and listen . . . Jack Benny was a master at this and so is Johnny Carson or Red Skelton; also Jonathan Winters.

Johnny Carson is especially good when a joke bombs. Pat Sajak (Wheel of Fortune) is really coming to the front of late as a great wit with timing. Let me clear this up at this point---I cannot compete with these guys, they are professionals from uptown; I'm just a country boy from the country. . . there is no comparison. I was poking fun at a guy one night at an engagement and was getting some good response at his expense when I realized he was being hit a little too hard (you can overdo it sometimes) so I tried to cap it off with a positive remark in his behalf and it backfired with more laughs. Here is what I said: "Sam over here has proven he has a sense of humor and is a good sport, also, I have heard he is a lot like Will Rogers in that he is a very good wit anyway." Without hesitation, a person in the audience remarked, "Well, we know that to be 'half true anyway'. . . now, that was perfect timing.

4. CLOSERS category examples: This category is very important in any talk, speech, or communication. Some speakers don't agree, but here is where I think we are worth our salt as professionals. Now is the time to be positive, witty, patriotic, or serious. Here is where I give them real "attitude." This is the opportune time to let them see that other side that you have and that other world that you are a part of. I do my best at this segment to give them a real zinger; sometimes I succeed. What happened to the example of "Closers?" . . . . Here they are: "Let me close tonight with a story. . . and I want to get really serious for a moment--years ago, two brothers, who happened to be bicycle mechanics from Ohio, decided to invent, or concoct, a machine that would fly. These men put everything they had into something they believed in . . . it was

bazaar, frightening, crazy and many other adjectives you can think of. . . but they believed. . .and that was the important thing. . .they had a plan on how to do it. . . that was also important, and they didn't mind the sacrifice which was also very important. . . and on that cool December morning in 1903, when they lifted off from Kill Devil Hills at Kitty Hawk, North Carolina, aviation history was made. The world has never been the same since. Nothing has had a greater impact than that great feat at Kitty Hawk, North Carolina. And, as I look around this room tonight, I see some of this same stuff that propelled the 'Wright Brothers' into immortality. . . and I challenge you along with myself to give everything you have for something you really believe in; construct a plan on how to do it; and don't mind the sacrifice to get it done. After all, this is America and we are Americans, and that is what we're all about."

Here's another: "A boy's lifetime dream was to become a professional baseball player. . . and in 1943, he made it all the way to the big leagues. He played for the St. Louis Browns professional baseball team. . . but he never started a game, never got a hit, didn't even finish out the first year at the majors, but, Pete Graves is an immortal and belongs up in Cooperstown in the Hall of Fame in my opinion, and the reason is simple. . . Pete Graves made it all the way to the big leagues with only one arm. . . He never considered what he did not have, but just took what he did have and went from there. You see, life is not being dealt the good hand, but taking the hand you were dealt and making the best of it. . . Your group reminds me of that attitude-the type of people who take what they have and use it to the best of their ability and go from there."

"Let me tell you a dumb story. . . did you know a bumblebee cannot fly?? Yes, that's right. A bumblebee cannot fly. . . aerodynamically, he just can't. . . his body is too big and his wings are too small for him to lift off. . . it's a scientific fact. . . but what does he do?? He flies!!! Why?? Number one, he can't read so he doesn't know he can't fly; he is 'intelligently ignorant.' There are some other people in history who were like the bumblebee. . . some of these are: Eli Whitney, a school teacher from Connecticut, a thousand miles from the cotton fields of the south, who invented the cotton gin; George Eastman, the Kodak King, revolutionized the family snapshot industry-- for years people thought the only camera in the world was a Kodak. George was a sound teacher. John D. Rockefeller sold produce in the streets.

The Duesenburg brothers were immigrant farmers--their cars are still priceless today. . John Deere revolutionized the common plow by creating a metal that midwestern land would not stick to. . . and C. Milo Jones, after being stricken with a stroke that left him paralyzed from the neck down, realized his brain was intact and in garbled tones told his sons how to mass produce piglet sausage that led to an empire. . . even today you still see 'Jones Meats' in the marketplace. All these people fall into the category of being 'intelligently ignorant.' We could all use some of it -- instead of trying to figure out how not to do something, just be too dumb to realize it won't work. . . and make it work."

Okay, these are just a few I use. . . there are hundreds of others out there somewhere for you to research and use with your own personality. . . I seem to be drawn to these type because of my own background and upbringing. You can find some "Closers" that seem more comfortable to your upbringing and background. Good Luck!!!!!

Where I Use Humor and
Material I've Categorized

Specifically, you'll use it everywhere in your communications. In each talk or speech, you'll use this material about every half minute or so-or at least every other story or byline. You could use it less, depending upon your personality or disposition or the type of audience. Again, as we said in the beginning, you must be comfortable first, then your audience will be comfortable.

Let us discuss that "talk" or "speech" right now. As you probably already know - any presentation comes in three major parts: the opening, the body, and the close. Me personally, I stray somewhat from that format; but not much. The "opening" or "introduction" of a speech is there to outline subject material or what you are about to talk about. The "body" is to discuss or bisect the material, and the "close" is to summarize. Just like the old professor at Grambling College said, "I'm gonna tell you what I'm gonna tell ya; then I'm gonna tell ya; then I'm gonna tell ya I told ya." That is essentially the makeup of a presentation, speech, talk or address. Here is where I deviate from that format. I open my talks with anything I feel necessary to get the audience's attention and "set the stage" and I try to my best to do it with Impact. I have, and this is certainly not unique, fallen on the way to the podium (deliberately, of course) just to gain immediate empathy. Also, I have come up with a story "off the wall" just to get the crowd rolling-myself included.

Now, let's talk about the body of the speech; here is where I am different somewhat in that the "body" of my talks are sometimes totally unrelated to the opening-- bears no similarity or relativity at all. (Unless I am addressing the PTA, SEA or the NEA, then I try to stick.) I use the body, and I suggest you do also for whatever will make your talk or speech most dramatic or entertaining. . . remember, you have got to keep them listening. You have to remember that my talks are for entertainment - not to educate - that explains why I am so unorthodox in my deliveries.

My wife left me a note saying I do educate in an unorthodox way, whether I am willing to admit it or not. She feels you can get more education through to people by humor than by any other method of teaching. Perhaps she's right or a little biased; but in any event, we know why teaching is not done with humor - most people, up until this book just couldn't do it with Humor!!! Right? Right!

Boy, I can remember the boring classes I sat through knowing there was a better way. Also, I realize everybody is not motivated to learn by humor, but very few fit into that category. When was the last time you heard a student come home raving about how "great" a certain teacher was and how "fun" she or he was with the subject matter. Then there are those educators who rationalize their methods by saying, "Educating people is Serious!"

To those I say, "Yes," the material is "serious" but the method of transferring that material can be variable to humorous. So, yes, you can use humor to teach. Whether it be public education, church, business, office, and wherever. Sprinkle the method with humor and you'll find it's like cooking - it doesn't seem right unless you sprinkle a little seasoning or spices into it. Here's the only test I can suggest - try it! See what the results are, get the opinion of your students or associates. But please!! You owe it to yourself to try it just one time. The application is the same as a talk or speech because that's what you are really doing. Take note sometimes of politicians; it's amazing how much humor they use; also TV evangelists, and other clergy are using humor more and more. After all, it keeps audiences listening and sometimes laughing.

Now, let's talk about that close or end to the speech.

You may want to summarize somewhat or a lot, it's up to you. I personally do not summarize a great deal unless the presentation is for an exam or a test. Otherwise, why bother them with the same material. The close should be used to challenge the audience or to rattle their emotions. Also, you may want to drive home a point with impact. I usually let them know I am closing by remarking that a closing story is coming. This story or quip should be informative or provocative or both. . . but should always be challenging. In Chapter 6 you will find some "closers" and some more in Chapter 7. Should none of these suit you then use all the secret places for material I gave you in Chapter 2.

Some more anecdotes. . .

"The difference between "She's good looking" and "She's looking good" is approximately 30 years and 30 pounds."

"You can stay young forever if you live honestly, eat slowly, get lots of sleep, work hard, worship faithfully and lie about your age."

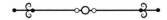

Wayne Hopper

A CLOSE UP OF LAUGHING MARKS. . .
IS ANYTHING <u>THAT</u> FUNNY?

Brothers Laughing

FROM L TO R:

CLAUDE, WILL, MONROE, STEVE, &
WAYNE LAUGHING, AS USUAL,
THIS ONE PROBABLY ABOUT THE
HOMEMADE FOOTBALL.

WE ALL GREW UP ON THIS OLD HOBBY
HORSE; 60 - 82 YEARS LATER OUR
GRANDCHILDREN ARE USING IT...

THESE ARE 4 OF 24 GRANDCHILDREN
OF WAYNE AND SHIRLEY.

NOTICE THE OLD HOMEPLACE
IN THE BACKGROUND

Wayne Hopper

SOPHOMORE PHOTO AT
EAST CAROLINA UNIVERSITY
IN 1958.
HE'S STILL ODDLY SHAPED.
A SMILE DON'T EVEN FIT HIM!

Getting It All Together

First - Speaking is a terrifying experience, especially right before your introduction when you haven't even said anything yet. You sit there, putting on the face, or you pace the back of the hall, mentally envisioning everything that can go wrong, you remember "Murphy's Law," if anything can go wrong, it will go wrong. It's like waiting in a dentist's office with a painful tooth, it's like waiting in a doctor's office knowing he's gonna massage your prostrate. Okay-What have I done here? I've almost discouraged you from ever waiting to make a talk or presentation or speech - right? Wrong!! I have to mention these things I've just mentioned. Why? Because regardless of how many times we do it or how good we are, all of the above things happen each time we deliver. And the fact that you're uptight is what will make the appearance so great. You start out "Human" and you'll end up "Human" and that's what makes it all so tremendous!!!

Second - One of the most debilitating thoughts that can cross your mind is: "What if they don't like me???" You can become terrorized by these thoughts!! What if my hands shake?? My voice cracks? etc., etc. These thoughts are dangerous and can be tuned out rather easily if you just use good common sense to do it. It has <u>all</u> happened to <u>all</u> speakers at some time during their career.

John Wooden, the legendary basketball coach of UCLA, never mentioned the word "win" to his players. He encouraged them only to do their best. His philosophy was that if you do your best and you are more skilled than your opponent, you will win. If you do your best and the opponent beats you, he deserved to win all along. There was nothing you could do about it. However, if you worry about winning, it invariably will prevent you from doing your best. Then an unworthy adversary may well beat you. Speakers, too, should adopt that attitude. Prepare well and do your best, but leave the audience's work to the audience. Don't worry about failure--you have got to know you will succeed and you will. Remember the "old" Murphy's Law: "Expect the best and you'll get the best." There is also a quote from U.S. Anderson: "When the student is ready, the teacher will appear." The same applies here, "when the audience is ready, the speaker will appear." Let the responsibility of the audience lay on the shoulders of the audience.

Third - Review in your mind what brought you there for the event in the first place. These people didn't invite you by picking your name out of the phone book. You deserve to be there and to speak on your subject. Remember all the past successes you have had with this particular talk already. The material that was good before will be better tonight. Think on positive things the entire evening; eliminate the negative things in your life--tune them out. I'll let you in on a little secret--I tape all my talks and on the evening or during the day before the event I will play that tape. On some occasions I have played them on the way to the engagement. Boy, is that an upper!! I'm ready to tear the place apart by the time I get there.

Take control of yourself at the event; don't let anyone get to you or your attitude. This happened to me once, where I let a person get to me and controlled my material for the night. You noticed I said <u>once</u>!!! I learn fast! I am like the cat that jumps on the hot stove, he never jumps on a hot stove again--in fact, he never jumps on a cold stove either. Be like that cat! Another suggestion I have for you--read Gene Ferret's book, especially the chapter on "establishing a Spirit of Fun at a speech." His book, How to Hold an Audience with Humor, is great.

Fourth - Know your audience!!!

Now, you'll never really know your audience until about five minutes into your program, but there are ways of getting to know them without a biased, slanted opinion, I mentioned previously in the chapter. You can ask the person who invites you - he'll usually give a good average run down of the makeup of your audience by age, sex and status. Usually he'll give you names that can be picked on a little. The host or hostess will also funnel you information about the group. You also may want to come early to the cocktail hour and meet some of the guests. Some groups you speak to you already know enough to speak well because of who they are.

Example: I spoke to a McDonald's (fast food) group not long ago and it was easy to find material. I started off by saying - I used to eat a lot at Burger King. You've heard of them haven't you? This caused the crowd to go wild. Try to speak from the audiences frame of reference, not yours. You don't offend, it's just fun for you.

Like the time the crowd was a rival of McDonald's and I said their sign said over 100 million because they had already used five pounds of meat. They loved it but knew it was just rivalry and fun, and I told them so.

I always poke a little fun at religious groups. I'll put Methodist against Baptist or Presbyterian or whatever. Here's a good one to use. We know Moses was not Baptist because the finance committee would have never agreed for him to make the trip. And we know he wasn't Methodist because they would have required scuba diving gear for the Deacons, Elders and Stewards. That credit goes to somebody else. . . . is not that good. Sometimes I pick on my wife--she wanted me to get religion--I said "how much??" She said "enough to zip me up, scratch my back, take out the garbage and stuff like that." (That's Bob Harrington's favorite.) Most of your material should fit any audience. Material in the "frame of reference" of any audience should be the bulk of your material. My wife says to me: "Ok, Ok, I'll admit I spend a lot of money; name one other extravagance." Usually, somebody in the audience has a wife, or is one--so, wife jokes are usually in any audience "frame of reference." At a law officers convention or lawyers meeting or convention, you can use this one: "The trouble with justice nowadays is that it is not admissible in a court of law." At a senior citizens event you may use these: "By the time you get it all together, you're unable to carry it." Another, "I turned 94 yesterday and did it without jogging--mature citizens say a marathon serves a very useful purpose--running 26 miles keeps them from doing something even dumber." For a farmers event or agricultural community you can use this: "A tractor was seen on the side of the road with a 'For Sale' sign on it. It was an unusual tractor in that it had no seat or steering wheel. . . upon closer inquiry, the man selling it says: 'It's for the farmer who lost his butt and don't know which way to turn.'" (American Airlines Magazines) I was introduced to a very successful man and out of curiosity, I asked him his formula for success--He responded: GOOD JUDGMENT." I asked, "How do you get that?" He responded: "Experience." So I ask, "How do you get that?" He responded, "BAD JUDGEMENT!!!!" There is a tremendous point to that one for use in "Point Illustrators."

At this particular time let me point out the importance of picking a "focal" point in the audience (face). This can make you or break you when you first begin to speak in public. It is a must to find that friendly face or laughing face in the crowd and focus on it until you get rolling or as you need to get rolling again from time to time. As time goes on you can pick out the person in the audience who is not responding to anything. You can challenge this person and try to break them. Sooner or later you do.

There is plenty of material available everywhere and if you are like me you can't afford a writer, so you have to dig it out yourself. Bennett Cerf says joke books are a must; on the other hand, Gene Perret says don't use joke books except as a last resort or not at all. I say you've got to have material and you need it from wherever you can get it. Not everyone is a Will Rogers who was a comedy writer who used his own material. In Will's case, not only was he comical, he was a great wit-that's funny with intelligence. He is also known as one of the, if not the, greatest communicators known to man.

Even more anecdotes. . .

"Women, I find, are never satisfied. They're either trying to put on weight, take it off or rearrange it."

"I go on working for the same reason that a hen goes on laying eggs."

"Men have a much better time of it than women. For one thing, they marry later, for another, they die earlier."

"A girdle is a device which prevents figures from being facts."

"I don't object to my wife having the last word; in fact, I'm kinda use to it. But sometimes I think she will never get to it."

"The way I figure it, an expert is a fellow who can take something you already know and make it confusing."

"Somebody asked Daddy one day if the eggs he was selling were fresh eggs - he turned to one of his sons and said, "Feel those eggs and see if they're cool enough to sell."

Some Material

In this chapter, I want to give you a respectable list of "OPEN-ERS," "POINT ILLUSTRATORS," "PURE ENTERTAINMENT STORIES" (Breakers), and "CLOSERS." But, before I do that, let me give one little warning--Don't get too high and mighty before the audience. You should never tell people why you deserve to be up there--they'll decide that - they're the audience! And always, always brag about them--even if you have to exaggerate; brag and compliment--they're human, they will reciprocate, believe me. Frank Sinatra never walks out and says, "I am great!" Please respond accordingly. We can learn from this. You don't have to say that you are a star or even imply that you are--the audience will decide that. And another thing--never, I mean never, work to one side of the room. Now I know every speaker has a favorite side; but, you can't afford the luxury. . . don't fall into that trap. Me personally, I'm near sighted, so both sides are the same to me--I am fortunate in that respect. Just remember to concentrate on working the entire assemblage. At this point, you're probably saying I'm confused--you just said in the previous chapter to use a focal point (face). What if this focal point is not in the middle? Well, the focal point is to glance at from time to time for reassurance, not to home-in on. I'm happy to make that clear.

A speech, talk, or presentation is actually a dialogue. You're addressing a crowd but they are communicating with you also. They are communicating with you by what we call "non-verbal" communications. This is good because "words" are very poor vehicles to transfer thought. So, tune in with your audience. Involve them and concentrate on them a lot--forget yourself. Would you be shocked if I said: ninety percent of all communications between human beings is non-verbal- only ten percent is done with words. Body language is very important. An entire book has been dedicated to that one subject--"Body Language." Remember "silent movies?" Very little had to be explained when watching and very few words were used.

Some speakers involve the audience a lot. . .some keep a steady flow of people involved. . . asking questions, having them stand up, raise hands, coming up on stage, etc. . . . . this is called real audience involvement; when you can keep a parade going. I have not perfected this type of method yet. It sounds great and

I have seen it done and the audience seems to enjoy it. My suggestion on "audience involvement" is to go slow with it until you feel comfortable doing it. . .you must be good at controlling this type of presentation. I ask for a couple of names before the talk and try to poke fun at them as an "Audience Involvement" method or I will ask the audience a question for response. As time goes on, maybe I'll be good enough to keep a parade going.

Another point I want to mention, and I should treat this so lightly: "Let the audience know where the jokes are." This can be done several ways, through inflections, mannerisms, pauses or just right-out tell them. . . develop a form and perfect it.

Okay now, on with the material. . .this should be good stuff!

"OPENERS"--remember my openers are not conducive with the normal opening of a speech, I just dive right in with:

1. "If I can get just one laugh tonight; if I can make one person laugh out there; or just smile a little; if I can get just one chuckle; then I'll know my performance was a flop."

2. A tractor salesman was riding down a country road when he looked over on a hillside and spotted a farmer plowing a bull. Now, he stopped that pickup he was driving on a dime, jumped out, ran thru a field, forded a creek, ran up the hill to where the older farmer was plowing and breathlessly said: "Mr. Farmer, this is the luckiest day of your life!" The farmer asked: "Why's that, sonny?" The salesman replied: "Why I'm a tractor salesman, I've got tractors that could plow in one day for as far as the eye can see; why, it'll take forever to plow that much with this bull." The old farmer replied: "Let me tell you something, sonny, I have a brand new tractor sitting up there under the shed. What I'm trying to accomplish here today is to teach this bull there is something in this world besides eating and sex " I follow this story up by saying: "There is something in this world besides what you folks do and are doing and I certainly hope I can add to it just a little."

3. " I come here tonight with some new medical information I am sure you will find both informative and amusing. Doctors have now discovered that when women suppress laughter it has a tendency to travel down the body and broadens the hips--in men, it gets trapped in the cavity of the body and creates gas." I follow this up by commenting that nobody suppress their laughter tonight.

4. "A college professor once told his entire class, and I hap-

pened to be in that class, that if you repeated something eight or ten times, it's yours. So on the way up to the podium tonight I repeated 'you are a star' eight or ten times. . . ."

5. " A person's mind starts when he is born and to different respects continues to work until he gets up to make a speech. . . ."

6. A crusty old Virginia famer was approached one day by an eager young salesman who was peddling a set of books on scientific agriculture. The old farmer was a difficult prospect. "What do I want them books for?" he scowled. "If you had these books, sir," the salesman pointed out, "you could farm twice as good as you do now." "Hells bells, son," roared the old farmer, "I don't farm half as good as I know how now."

7. Old man Fowler, down in Lawrenceville, Virginia, took his young son on an expedition to buy a new cow years ago. The father gave is prospective purchase a going over from head to foot, poking, probing, and pinching the animal very thoroughly. "You see, son," he explained, "when you buy a cow you want to be sure it's a sound one." The boy nodded approval. A week later the boy came running breathlessly to his father in a distant corner of the farm. "Come quick, Pa." he entreated. "A traveling salesman pulled up behind the barn, and it looks like he's going to buy sister."

8. I was telling my wife tonight that a humorist sometimes has a frustrating job. . .he does his job, the people are amused for a time. . . he leaves and the audience has received nothing specifically-no new found knowledge, no new learning system, no new gossip, probably no new enlightenment, etc. Now, I worked hard preparing my material, organized it, delivered it. . . and you'll receive nothing. My wife says, "Don't worry, just remember our honeymoon!" (self depreciation).

9. At my last engagement, we had finished dinner and dessert and the crowd was sitting around enjoying coffee. The toastmaster leaned over to me and asked, "Wayne, do you want them to enjoy themselves a little longer or do you want to do your speech now?" I know the gentleman meant well, of course. (Self deprecation is always a hit.)

10. A young minister was vacationing in the ski resort up at Wintergreen, Virginia, when he learned that a lady guest of the hotel, recently arrived from Boston, was gravely ill. Anxious to cheer her up he paid a courtesy call, murmured a wish for her

speedy convalescence, and concluded, "I should like to say a brief prayer for your recovery before I leave." The sick lady rallied at once and snapped, "That won't be necessary young man; I am being prayed for in Boston." I follow that up by saying "Anybody who wants to pray for me this evening, go right ahead."

I sincerely hope these few "openers" will give you an idea or two for your own research. You certainly may use these since I received them from somebody else myself. Chapter 7 will give you a few more.

"POINT ILLUSTRATORS"

"A man was in New York at La Guardia Airport waiting for his flight and had a little time to kill. So, he ambles over to a "Fate and Weight Machine," drops a nickel and out comes a message on a little piece of paper. It read: 'Your name is Wayne Hopper, you weigh 190 pounds and you're going to Boston on the 220.' Well, the guy couldn't believe it. He messed up his hair a bit, rearranged his coat and stepped back on the machine, dropped in a nickel and out came the piece of paper that read: 'Your name is still Wayne Hopper, you still weigh 190 pounds and you're still gonna catch the 220 to Boston.' Well, this was incredible. The man goes into the bathroom, changes clothes, combs his hair, parts it on the opposite side, goes back on the machine, drops in a nickel and out comes the piece of paper with the message: 'Your name is still Wayne Hoper, you still weight 190 pounds, but you just missed the 220 to Boston!!!

Okay, so what's the message?? It is simple: Cicero said it over one thousand years ago: "More is lost by indecision than by wrong decision." Some people just can't make a decision when it is staring them in the face that all is well. Just make a decision - you only have to be right fifty-one percent of the time - you can be wrong forty nine percent and still be successful.

Another one: An old man sat at the gates of an ancient city greeting travelers. Time and again the people would ask the old man: "What kind of people live in this city?" The old man always answered with this question: "What kind of people live there in the place from whence you came?" And the people would say, "They were wicked people there, sinful, very bad, thieves, etc." And the old man would answer: "The same type of people live here!!!" On another occasion when new people would ask him what type of people live in this city and he would ask them the same question: "What type of people live in the place from whence you came?" They would respond: "They were good, positive, terrific neighbors, etc." Then the old man would answer: "The same type of people live here." Here's the point and I am sure you've already got it. Whatever it is you are looking for or expect, can be found wherever you go.

Those two were more of the serious nature. Now let me give you one of a humorous nature.

"During World War II, our air corps pilots would do training missions out of Georgetown, South Carolina. They would fly out over the Atlantic and practice with 'live' bombs. On this particular day when they released their bombs, one got stuck and didn't release, it was just hanging by a thread. The pilot did not know it however, and started back to base. As he flew over this farm where a little old lady was milking the cow, the bomb released right over the cow, landed right on top of the cow and blew it to smithereens. . . left the little old lady holding the bag." Now this is a favorite of Zig Ziglar, author of 'See You at the Top'. He follows it up by saying, "That's what happens to most of us in life when it comes to success; we're left holding the bag."

Here's another: This is an oldie: A drunk was on his way home one night after carousing around and took a shortcut through the cemetery and fell into a freshly dug grave. He clambered around for awhile, wore out most of his fingernails and toenails trying to get out to no avail. He finally sat down in the corner of the thing exhausted. It wasn't long after that another drunk fell in the grave. He didn't see the first man, but began to try to get out. The first drunk then said: "You can't get out of here." And out the second guy went just as slick as you've ever seen.

The point here is: "With proper motivation, a person can do things he never thought possible."

"PURE ENTERTAINMENT STORIES" and "BREAKERS"

These stories can be your own "best" stories and can always be replenished on a daily basis. Their purpose is purely entertainment and nothing else.

It has been observed: "At twenty a woman has the face God gave her. At thirty she has a face representing the goods on the drugstore counter. At forty she has a face which displays the skill of her hairdresser and masseuse. At fifty her face represents the way her husband treats her. But at sixty, she has the face she gave herself." The point: More than strikes the eye goes into the making of a face. Like the molding of character, the making of a countenance is the work of a lifetime. What counts takes time.

As an old gentleman reached his 100th birthday, he was asked by a newspaper reporter: "To what do you attribute your longevity?" Thoughtfully he replied, "Well, I never smoke, I never drank liquor, I never overate, and I always rise at six in the morning." "But," countered the reporter, "I had an uncle who did the same and he only lived to be eighty. How do you account for that??" "He didn't keep it up long enough," came the centenarian's terse reply. So what's the point. . . The lasting things that count, last as long as we last at them.

An experience painter had a visitor in his studio to ask how long it took to paint a picture he had just completed. He replied. "Two hours to put on the paints, but forty years to learn how." What's the point to this story? A lifetime of devotion goes into the dedication demanded to do anything noteworthy and worthwhile.

Two of our children are almost the same age and always somebody is asking if they are twins. On one occasion when this was asked, one of them replied: "Yes, we are sisters, one of us is adopted, but I forgot which one."

My brother wanted to attend the small college of Elon. He could play football pretty good and heard that they had a really good team so he called and got a scout for the team on the phone. My brother says, "I'm a pretty good player. I run the 100 in less than ten seconds. I tackle so hard that five opposing players got broken legs this season. I can pass into the wind and hit a running receiver seventy yards away. I made twelve touchdowns in two games running up the middle. In my grades I stand near the top of the class." The drooling scout exclaimed, "That's great, but surely you have some weakness." "Well, yes," confided my brother, "I am inclined to exaggerate now and then."

After many years of coaching Little League baseball, I had never heard such an optimistic remark as I did during one game when we were at our dismal worst. A man had stopped to watch the game and asked one of my players: "What's the score?" The player, "Thirty-five to nothing." The man said, "Whose favor?" The player, "Theirs." The man, "Rather a one-sided game, isn't it?" "No sir," replied the boy, "we haven't had our inning yet."

Time and again a youngster had fallen as he was trying to learn to skate on ice. A sympathetic spectator who had been watching him said kindly, "Sonny, you're getting all bumped up. I wouldn't stay on the ice and keep falling down so; I'd just come off and watch the others." The courageous little tyke answered, "I didn't get these new skates to give up with; I got them to learn how with." There's a tremendous point to this one. . . .

Little is remembered longer than that which is expressed in the briefest compass possible to convey the message adequately. The Lord's Prayer contains 56 words; the Ten Commandments, 297; the Declaration of Independence, 3,000; and yet a government order regulating the price of cabbage took 26,911 words. The military cemetery at Gettysburg was dedicated in 1863 with the delivery of two addresses. One speaker orated for two hours and he spoke eloquently, but few remember even the name of Edward Everett. The other spoke for two minutes and he spoke simply, but ever since, the name of Abraham Lincoln has been associated with the occasion.

I'll give you a few other entertaining stories because I promised I would. . . not because they are great or anything like that.

"A biography of Chief Justice Salmon P. Chase, who headed the Supreme Court in the crucial years from 1864 to 1872, reveals that he was as agile-tongued and as irresistible in the drawing room as he was on the bench. A few years after the Civil War ended, the chief justice was introduced to a flaming beauty from the border of North Carolina and Virginia. "I must warn you," she told him archly, "that I am a Rebel who has not been reconstructed." The gallant judge promptly responded, "Madame, reconstruction in your case-even in the slightest degree would be nothing short of sacrilege."

Mrs. Russell Crouse of Richmond was interviewing a new nurse and asked why she had left her last post. "I didn't like the set up," said the nurse, frankly. "The child was backward and the father was forward."

The Sunday School teacher asked Willie, "If you had a large, good apple and a small wormy one, and you were told to divide with your brother, which would you give him?" Willie answered, "Do you mean my big brother or my little one?"

A moonshiner in Franklin County, Virginia, was caught red-handed by a posse of revenue agents. The moonshiner, despite his seventy years and a long gray beard, tore himself loose from the sheriff's grasp, and headed cross country with the speed of a gazelle. The sheriff, a kindly and lazy soul, marveled at the old boy's agility, and said, "Let's let him go."

Five days passed, however, and the moonshiner failed to return.

Just as his relatives and neighbors were concluding he had died someplace, he stumbled home. "Where have you been Clem?" they asked. The moonshiner simply replied: "I been coming back."

A lady from Farmville descended upon a dentist there for the fifth time to command him to grind down her false teeth again. "I tell you they don't fit," she insisted. "Okay," said the dentist reluctantly. "I'll do it one last time." But by every test, they should fit your mouth perfectly as they are." Who said anything about my mouth?" snapped the lady. "They don't fit in the glass."

The classic doctor's story is about the fine old country doctor in southwest Virginia who had neither time nor inclination to dun patients for payment. He died in his second story office one morning and one of his few worldly possessions was the wooden sign that had stood on his lawn for fifty years or more. His loyal patients would have liked nothing better than to buy him an imposing tombstone, but they were just as poor as he was. After his funeral-therefore, they uprooted the wooden sign and lovingly planted it on his grave. It read: "Dr. Davis, Upstairs."

In a small town in North Carolina, the sheriff doubles as the vet. In the middle of one cold night he received an emergency call. "Do you want me as sheriff or vet?" he inquired. "Both," came the agitated reply. "We can't get our dog's mouth open and there's a burglar's rear in it."

That should be enough pure stories as an example of what you need. Be sure to use these - I have and naturally got them from somebody else. Chapter 7 has more.

"CLOSERS" - this is normally my specialty, but sometimes these are very difficult to put on paper. For me it is much easier to do from up front.

The story is told of a General "Marion," that's all I know. Around the twelfth of August, 1780, he received a summons from a brave band of Patriots near Williamsburg, Virginia, to join them and become their leader.

Governor Rutledge of South Carolina, conferred on him a General's commission, and placed him in command in that part of the state known as Linch's Creek. This was the beginning of the famous and deathly feared by the British, "Marion's Brigade." This brigade grew, and to serve with "Marion" was esteemed the highest privilege to which a man could aspire who wished to serve his country. "Marion was known as the "Swamp Fox" and would rake havoc on supplies and munitions of the British. He would personally lead his troops in these attacks that never saw a failure, no vigilance could guard against his attacks; no persevering efforts could force him to a conflict when the chances of loss were against him.

While at Snow's Island, there was an exchange of prisoners. A young British officer was sent from Charleston to complete the arrangements with "Marion." He was brought into the camp blindfolded and when unblindfolded couldn't believe his eyes as he saw before him "Marion," small in stature, slight in person and beyond, his officers and men rudely costumed under the shadows of the tall trees of the swamps. The young officer was astonished. Was this the man and brigade whose mere name had been so famous and feared and would strike terror in the hearts of the Tories??? After business was over, the officer was invited to stay for dinner. He did so. Sweet potatoes smoking from the ashes were placed upon a piece of bark and set before the General and his guest. "Doubtless this is an accidental meal," said the bewildered officer, "You live better than this in general???"

"No," was the reply, "we often fare much worse."

"Then I hope at least you draw noble pay to compensate?"

"Not a cent, sir." replied the man, "Not a cent."

The officer reported at Charleston that he had seen an American General and his officers, without pay and almost without clothes, living on roots and drinking water--all for liberty!!! "What chance have we against such men?" he said. This officer resigned his commission and never afterwards served during the war.

This is a good example of a *Wake Up, America* closer. At this point you ask the audience, "Are we still that type of America that would sacrifice just a few conveniences for liberty!!!?????As those men did?

"CLOSING STORY"--Former President Nixon, in an address, made these remarks: "Two hundred years ago, we were not the wealthiest or greatest nation on earth, but we had the "spirit" to become that. . . .Now, today, we have become the greatest and wealthiest nation on earth, but we have lost the 'spirit'. . . .

This is another good example of *Wake Up, America* closer. At this point you challenge the audience, "Have we really lost that 'spirit'?"

"A HUMOROUS CLOSER"--As you slide down the banister of life, be careful you don't get a splinter in your career.

Korea

WAYNE... IN KOREA

Wayne & Shirley Hopper

WITH TEN WONDERFUL CHILDREN.
EACH ONE A SPECIAL BLESSING. . .
IN THEIR OWN WAY OF COURSE...

Hoppers 48th Anniversary

WAYNE - STUMBLING AND FUMBLING AT THE 48TH ANNIVERSARY CONCERT AT EDEN, NC. THOSE FANTASTIC, GOOD-LOOKING HOPPER BROTHERS AND CONNIE IN BACKGROUND TRYING TO BAIL HIM OUT. . . PRETENDING HE IS ENTERTAINING...

NOTICE:
· PANTS ARE UP UNDER HIS ARMPITS
· ONLY HOPPER WEARING GLASSES

Yokahama, Japan

WAYNE ON R&R IN
YOKAHAMA, JAPAN

DID I TELL YOU HOW
I GOT MY FIRST SUIT?

Virginia

HOPPER'S OLDEST SISTER, VIRGINIA,
AT THE 48TH ANNIVERSARY.
SHE WAS A GOD SENT WOMAN!!
AIN'T SHE BEAUTIFUL?

Funny Stuff: Part Two

During World War II, the order came out that gasoline was going to be rationed. This concerned my daddy a little so he summoned my brother Monroe to take a five-gallon can of gasoline out behind the barn and bury it for the future reserve and keep it hidden in case of government inspection. About an hour later, Monroe came around from behind the barn with shovel in hand and yelled, "What do you want me to do with the empty five-gallon can???"

A man by the name of Jack Hawkins, of Madison, had been known by some to leave his son's business (billiard parlor, snack bar with beer) a little inebriated sometimes. Well, on this one particular night, there was a dreadful fog hanging on the entire county. Jack, not being able to see where he was going, finally found a set of taillights and latched onto them with hopes of the other driver leading him out of the fog. Everything went fine until the other driver came to an abrupt stop and Jack plowed right into his rear end, yelling, "Why didn't you signal you were going to stop??" The other driver yelled back, "I don't usually signal when I am stopping in my own garage!!!"

A cousin of mine, Tee Pot Fry, from nearby Stoneville, North Carolina, was baseball coach at Oakridge Military Institute. He played twelve years of minor league baseball for the Red Sox at nearby Reidsville. He was also a fanatic on hitting and players that could hit. One day Coach Cure called him all the way from Madison - "I just saw a pitcher that will set all kinds of records for you," he declared. "He's got a blinding fastball, perfect control, and a dipsy-doodle drop that fades out of site. I saw him pitch a perfect game today - no hits, twenty-two strike outs. . . only one guy hit a foul ball over fifty yards." "To heck with the pitcher," said Tee Pot, "What's the name of the guy who hit that foul???

The football coach asked me, "Hopper, where are most football games lost?" I replied, "Right here at Madison High, Coach!!"

The slowest train in the world had to be the old Norfolk and Western from Roanoke to Winston-Salem. A lady on the train, during one wretched trip, approached the conductor and told him she had to get off, she was going to have a baby. He told her she shouldn't have gotten on the train in that condition. She replied, "I didn't!!"

A local minister dropped into the barber shop for a quick shave and had the misfortune to choose a chair attended by one of our more astute barbers suffering from a hangover. His breath nearly asphyxiated the poor minister and to cap it all off, the barber took a huge nick out of the minister's chin. "You see," said the minister, "what comes from intoxicating liquor?" "Yep," agreed the barber, "it sure makes the skin tender."

There's the story of a hometown woman who told her husband, "Be an angel and let me drive." He did - and he is.

Hamp Wilson was stopped by the State Police near Madison and given a ticket for doing seventy-five miles per hour. Hamp asked the trooper: "Couldn't you make it ninety an hour officer, I'm trying to sell this car to a young man."

The story is told of a Madisonian who drove all the way to Los Angeles without incident, but hit the freeway with all of its complex overpasses, underpasses and cloverleaves. Finally, as luck would have it, he spotted another Madisonian with his wife and four children in the car with him. He yelled, "Mister, can you help a neighbor out? I've been trying to get to the Civic Center for six hours and I wind up here at this spot every time."

"You're asking the wrong man, brother," replied the other guy with the wife and children, "I can't even get home from my honeymoon!"

A man from Walnut Cove was constantly annoyed by motorists who drove past his house at excessive speeds. The wily old feller put a stop to that nonsense with a large sign he had erected that slowed drivers down to a very slow crawl. The sign read: PLEASE PROCEED WITH CAUTION. . . NUDIST CAMP CROSSING JUST AHEAD.

We had a neighbor farmer near our place whose wife went stark raving mad one morning. Well, they took her off to Camp Butner leaving her husband scratching his head in perplexity. "I'm danged if I cain figger what's gotten into the old girl," he said. "She ain't been out of this house in thirty-two years!"

We had two farmers in the neighborhood named Landreth, father and son, who always tried to outdo each other with complaints or tales about their crops. At the local store one night the father said, "Never did see hay so short as mine this year." The son spoke up and said, "Yep, it was so short, we had to lather it to mow it."

We lived in a community where the only telephone service was a five-party line. That means any of five families could possibly be listening in on conversations at any given time. All you had to do was pick up and if somebody was talking, you could just listen. I was listening in on a conversation once and so was another party, when suddenly the other party abruptly threw the receiver down. At that time a person remarked to her party, "How about that, somebody just hung up on us."

An EX-LAX salesman came thru our area one cold day in December. The family was killing hogs and the salesman got all wrapped up in the activity of things. Well, an old fellow around sixty-five, always the curious type, proceeded to see what he had in his bag sitting there on the kitchen table. He found what he thought were some chocolate samples and proceeded to eat thirty-two of them. The salesman discovered the thirty-two wrappers (empty) after he left the household and didn't get back to the area for about four days. He was concerned that maybe it had caused some ill effects and wanted to check it out. As he passed the outside bathroom, he saw the old man sitting in there with the door open. He waved but the old man did not wave back. Thinking this was a little odd, he proceeded up the hill to the house and was greeted by the family. The salesman said he passed Grampa down there in the John but he didn't wave back or show any response. The family sadly exclaimed, "Grampa's been dead for three days now - we're just waiting for his bowels to stop moving so we can bury him."

We have a retired Air Force pilot in our neighborhood in Virginia. He served in World War II, test piloted one of the first B-29's and piloted General McArthur around at one time. I must add that he is well known in aviation circles. His nickname was "Squeaky."

This is a story that is told about him and to this writing I have not been able to confirm it.

It seems during the war when there was a lot of island hopping, "our pilot" was based on this one particular island where the C.O. delighted in getting the pilots out of bed in the middle of the night, every night, for an alert. After it happened thirty-two nights in succession, "our pilot" got a great idea. . . . He got hold of a tame orangutan that hung around begging for food, dressed him in full uniform, and trained him painstakingly to run to the plane whenever the alert sounded. He'd climb in, close the plexiglass dome over his head, pull down his goggles, switch on the engine, turn over the propeller and keep his hand on the throttle until he heard the "all clear" signal.

It worked like a charm for weeks. One night, however, the "all clear" signal never sounded. "Our pilot" ran over to the field just in time to see his plane, with the orangutan at the stick, take off in perfect style. When the planes zoomed off, there were only two people left on the field - "our pilot" and the C.O. The C.O. gave "our pilot" a withering look and strode off not saying a word.

So, when people asked "our pilot" why he was the oldest Captain in the Corps, he didn't mind that. . . if it weren't for the fact that damn orangutan made it to Lieutenant Colonel. . . .

There was a crusty old country banker from near Wytheville who suddenly decided on his eightieth birthday to be candid when asked how he got started in the banking business. "Wasn't nothing to it," confessed the old fellow. "I just hung out a sign saying 'Bank'. First thing you know, a fellow comes along and deposits $100.00. Later on another deposits $200.00. By that time I was so confident I put in $10.00 of my own money."

When a local minister at a church there at home was asked how a man of the cloth could justify his habit of smoking cigars and a pipe, he replied calmly, "I cultivate my flowers and burn my weeds."

My sister and I were in the drug store one day waiting for a prescription. Suddenly, the druggist spotted someone he wanted to see and asked my sister to answer the phone if it rang. The phone rang. "Madison Drug," said my sister. "Do you have Streptomycin and Aureomycin?" Asked the voice at the other end. My sister scratched her head, then said, "Ma'am, when I said 'Madison Drug,' I told you everything I know!"

We had a few moonshiners in our community. In most cases, they made it strictly for medicinal purposes and usually got away with it. On some occasions a "still" would go overboard and that drew the Sheriff or Revenuers. On one occasion it got around that somebody was selling it. So a Revenue Agent was making his approach when suddenly a shot rang out and something grazed his left sleeve. The Agent, undaunted, continued forward when a second shot whistled thru his coattails. When a third shot punctured his hat and still failed to stop him, a voice from the woods sounded, "One more step, mister, and I begin to take aim."

Lowell Knight's daughter called him one night and wailed, "I'm afraid I've married a drinking man. All last night Oscar kept mumbling in his sleep, 'No, Sidney, no, I don't care if it is free, not one more drink for me'." Lowell interrupted wistfully, "Did Oscar happen to mention any address?"

Uncle John and Frank Oliver were weaving their way down a railroad track somewhat inebriated. "Gosh," complained one, "this is a long flight of stairs." The other countered, "I don't mind the stairs so much, it's the low hand rails that get me."

Zeb Williams started off the new year by reporting, "I slept like a log last night. I must have. I woke up in the fireplace."

Izzie Mae appeared at a cotillion in a new gown which her beau informed her looked just right on her. "Sho' nuff?", she purred, blushing. He replied, "Sho' does."

Busik's Department Store in Madison had a unique way of sending late notices for the people with arrears in their accounts. It read: "It has been said that a man who squeezes a dollar, never squeezes his wife. In looking into your account, it has occurred to us that your wife is not getting the attention she probably deserves."

Our child came home from school on Report Card Day and kept a firm clutch on his semester grades. "Maybe," he said, "I should explain the grading system to you first. 'A' means wonderful. 'B' means excellent, 'C' stands for alright, and 'D' is what I got.

A grandmother, visiting the family, was freshening up for dinner when one of her grandsons, about four years old, brought his puppy in to see her. She said, "I'm busy now, dear, wait for me downstairs." The grandson asked her tearfully, "Grandma, aren't you even going to speak to your grand-dog?"

Did you hear the one about the grandmother who, after sixteen grandchildren, had her tubes tied?

A young woman from Halifax, Virginia, had the good fortune of goin' on a five-day cruise around the Caribbean. She gave this account of her trip:

Monday:	The Captain saw me on deck and was kind enough to ask me to sit at his table for the rest of the trip.
Tuesday:	I spent the morning on the bridge with the Captain. He took my picture leaning against the "Passengers Not Allowed on the Bridge" sign.
Wednesday:	The Captain made proposals to me unbecoming an officer and a gentleman.
Thursday:	The Captain threatened to sink the ship unless I agreed to his proposals.
Friday:	I saved 800 lives today.

ABOUT CHILDREN

Our son, James, on the first day of preschool, was looking forward with wild excitement to his first day. When the great day dawned, he bounced out of bed at seven and was ready to go by seven fifteen. He was still enthusiastic when he got home that afternoon. The next morning, however, when mom woke him at seven thirty, James wasn't quite so happy. "What??" he protested angrily, "Have I got to do it again??"

We enjoyed a huge fireplace in our home at Richmond and enjoyed fetching wood for it occasionally. At one cold snap, it caught me without wood, but I knew where they sold it by the wheelbarrow load, so we went on down there. (Bill, my oldest son but only ten at the time, and I). The man had several wheelbarrows lined up there at the station and told us to pick out one. Finally, I said, "That one." Bill was instructed to load the thing up in the station wagon. I went in to pay and when the station owner and I returned, Bill had the entire wheelbarrow full of wood pulled into the station wagon. How he did it I'll never know, but the owner fell down laughing.

We'd visit Granma and Granpa Hopper often down at their farm in North Carolina. On this one occasion our daughter, Deidrea, was observed perched precariously on the peaked roof of one of the barns. Somebody asked her what she was doing up there. She covered the situation perfectly. She called down: "I'm trying not to fall off."

Our most temperamental was Barbara, who raised tantrums every time she was told it was time for bed. "I hate bed." she yelled one night. "If I took bed in school it would be my worst subject."

We got a cute note from Sandra's teacher when she was in the fifth grade. The teacher asked, "Who said, 'God's in His Heaven, all's right with the world'?" Sandra answered, "Mrs. God."

Crystal, when seven years old, was invited to a party and had a spat with another guest and was sent home in disgrace. When she got home she found her cat had been run over on the highway. By then she burst into tears and wailed, "This is the worst day I have ever been to."

Our kids visited relatives for periods of time during the summer. One particular summer, Victoria was the guest and field hand of an uncle. On the first night, the aunt took her to a lovely guest room with a wide, spotless, cool bed and said: "Victoria, this is all yours." Victoria burst into tears. "I want to sleep in a regular bed," she sobbed. . ."one with four or five kids in it."

I took Elizabeth, about three years old at the time, with me early one morning to vote. I carried her right into the voting booth with me. After I pulled down a number of levers, I asked her, "See how it's done? "Yes, Daddy." she replied, with her eyes shining, "Now where's the bubble gum??"

I tried to always send the kids off to school the first day with a note that read: "The opinions expressed by this child are not necessarily those of (her) father's side of the family."

I overheard a tired-looking mother, entering the supermarket with her four boisterous youngsters, ask the clerk: "Haven't you got some brand of cereal that will zap their energy??"

An ad in the Madison Messenger: "Encyclopedia Britannica, complete set, for sale cheap, never used. <u>My wife knows everything</u>!"

A fellow named Red White in Rustburg asked the barber: "How much is a haircut?"

Barber: "Two fifty."

Red: "How much is a shave?"

Barber: "One fifty."

Red: "Okay, shave off my hair."

"Here's an autograph of Mark Twain."

"All I see is an 'X'."

"Well, that is his Mark."

"Where is the Twain?"

"Down at the Station."

"I was troubled with athlete's foot only once. That was the time our right tackle on the football team caught me out with his girl."

Professor Swreath, at East Carolina, made his remark: "A fool can ask more questions than a wise man can answer." No wonder so many of us flunked his last exam.

Dr. Robert McMillion, of Winston-Salem, North Carolina, has compiled "A Coronary Dialogue," which contains the following excellent nuggets of advice:

A. Thou shalt consider losing thy temper a luxury to be indulged in sparingly.

B. Thou shalt not try to be a champion athlete after fifty.

C. Thou shalt take regular vacations.

D. Thou shalt keep thy alcoholic intake below the point where it may delude thee into thinking thou art a better man than thou ever were.

E. After a certain age, thou shalt not take unto thyself a young and frisky wife, nor even a reasonable facsimile thereof.

Old Colonel Beauregard was a devil with the ladies, still charming the daylights out of them at seventy-seven. In fact, on his seventy-seventh birthday, he adopted the practice of cutting a notch on his cane to mark each new conquest. That's what killed him on his seventy-eighth birthday. He made the mistake of leaning on his cane.

INTERESTING FACTS

Many people may wonder where the images of Christ originated. How did they come about since no one knows what Jesus looks like? "Head of Christ" is one of the most familiar paintings of Jesus seen around the world today. Since its first print in 1940, there have been over a half billion copies sold. But where did it come from? Warner E. Sallman (illustrator of religious magazines) was told in 1924 that he needed a picture for a deadline the following day. He was blank. He had NOTHING - nothing. After countless hours of thinking, he decided to go to bed. However, he suddenly awoke with "a picture of Christ in my mind's eye just as if it were on my drawing board." It was then that he sketched the "Head of Jesus" with long brown hair, neat beard, blue eyes... The picture known as we know it today. ("Uncle John's Bathroom Reader")

Maxwell House Coffee is named for a hotel in Nashville, Tennessee, where the coffee was so excellent, Teddy Roosevelt declared impulsively, "It's good to the last drop."

Mr. Heinz was selling many more than fifty-seven varieties when he registered his trademark in 1896. He just like the number fifty-seven.

Camel cigarettes came along in 1913 when Turkish tobaccos were in vogue. The original camel was a venerable dromedary named "Old Joe" who lumbered through Winston-Salem with a circus just when R.J. Reynolds was seeking a name for their new brand. Not sure they were right, they put "old Joe" on their package. The rest is history.

George Eastman was a sound teacher when he revolutionized the snapshot industry with the "Kodak." He just liked the letter "K," so he came up with a word that began and ended with it. The word means nothing - try telling that to millions of people who own one!!!

In the late 1930s, Chester Carlson had a revolutionary idea--an electrostatic printing process--which he tried to sell to the top mimeograph companies in America. Turned away time and again, he finally converted his kitchen into a workshop and went into business for himself. There was risk and a shortage of capital, but the tiny enterprise survived and prospered.

Today we know it as Xerox.

When F.W. Woolworth opened his first store, a merchant down the block resented the new competition and hung out a big sign reading, "I Have Been Doing Business In This Spot For Over Fifty Years." The next day Mr. Woolworth hung up a sign too. His read: "Established a Week Ago: No Old Stock."

Ray Kroch left Florida broke and with no overcoat. When he arrived in cold Chicago to work for an electric milkshake mixing machine company that had the first machine that would mix up more than one milkshake at the time. By selling these machines to hot dog and hamburger joints he met the McDonald brothers of California. They had a hamburger joint that could make a hundred hamburgers at a time. They guaranteed only one thing--fast service. Ray tried to get them to go nationwide under a franchise system not too accepted at that time. They refused, saying they loved the valleys of California. So, Ray did it for them and was extremely successful. He later bought them out and you and I know it today as just plain McDonalds hamburgers with over three billion sold.

OTHER TIDBITS

The story is told of a businessman in Madison who found a redemption check for a pair of shoes wedged into a crack in one of his desk drawers. Scotty's Shoe Shop took pride in their work and even though the receipt was ten years old, the businessman, as a joke, took the ticket and presented it to Scotty's son who had taken over the business after his father's death. The businessman said "I know it's been ten years, but it occurred to me you might just be able to find them." "Wait here, I'll go see," said an unsmiling Scotty Jr. He handed back the ticket in a few minutes, explaining casually, "They'll be ready Tuesday."

An antique shop up in Bedford featured an extensive collection of old snuff boxes. "They're handed down by my dear departed grandmother," explained the proprietor.. "Oh," nodded a customer, "your grandmother took snuff?" "Not at all," said the proprietor, "she took snuff boxes."

FACTS ON INSURANCE PEOPLE

One foot-weary insurance agent resorted to the telephone, and after 293 prospects had hung up on him, decided to do the bazaar. He dialed the richest man in town. "I don't suppose," he asked timidly, "you are in the market for some additional life insurance?"

"It happens that I am," was the reply, the surprising reply. "Would you like to come out here and write me a policy for a million dollars?"

"Excuse me, sir," stammered the agent, "I must have the wrong number."

Another agent, and a very optimistic one by nature, came home in jubilant fashion one night after about two hours with an ornery prospect. "No vague promises this time," he told his wife. "He says he will definitely buy a policy when hell freezes over."

People think "Lloyd's of London" is the most famous insurance company in the world. As a matter of fact, Lloyd's writes no insurance whatsoever. It is merely an association, whose members write policies strictly on their own.

Originally, Lloyd's was a London coffee shop, where marine underwriters would gather! In 1774, "Lloyd's Rooms" were moved to the Royal Exchange, and there a big bell was installed. For a hundred years, every important event has been announced via the tolling of this bell. It was salvaged from the frigate Lufine, sunk off the Netherland's coast in 1799 with a million pounds of gold bars and coins aboard.

Marine protection is only one facet of the business done by Lloyd's today. You can insure "Beautiful Legs," as by Betty Grable; "Jumps," as by Evil Knievel; "Faces," as by Brooke Shields.

And even "fleas," as in trained fleas. There was a gentleman who had his fleas insured and it was very costly because it could not be determined how old they were. His premium was $100 for each $500 worth of fleas.

This is the conversation of one formidable wife of a henpecked husband and an insurance agent. "Let me be sure if I've got this right. You say that if my husband dies within one year, I'll get the full seventy thousand dollars mentioned in the contract?" "Of course," said the agent. "And within even a month?" "Yes, madam." "And if he dies the day after I sign him up?" "Then madam," said the agent, snapping shut his briefcase, "I'm confident you'll get seventy thousand -- but they won't be dollars, they'll be volts!!"

A man told of being marooned on an uninhabited treeless island without a bite to eat.

"How did you survive?" inquired his friends.

"By luck," explained the man. "I had my insurance policy in my pocket and I found enough provisions to keep me going indefinitely."

The first thing a person learns in the insurance sales business--every need ain't a want!

Nine of ten people you meet make this remark: "I've got too much insurance now!!!" But never in the history of American insurance companies has there been a request not to pay the portion that was too much. The remark following a claims check is usually; "I wish it had been twice this much!!"

ON WALL STREET

Still on record and treasured at the New York Stock Exchange, is a request from a southern gentleman who wrote the exchange that he was coming north to sell some hogs and would like "to get a couple of seats for the stock exchange which ain't behind no post or around in some corner where you can't see what's going on. Our Uncle Charles says you fellows put on the best show in New York."

A friend of mine called long distance to New York and asked for the head of a Wall Street brokerage house, and once admitted to the inner sanctum, explained, "I have a really tough investment problem." We're here precisely for cases like yours," assured the broker, cheerfully. "Just what is the nature of your problem?" My friend said, "I haven't any money."

J.K. Galbraith, witty professor of economics at Harvard, explains in his book, *The Affluent Society*. "The nature of a vested interest has an engaging flexibility. In ordinary intercourse it is an improper advantage enjoyed by a political minority to which the speaker does not himself belong. When the speaker enjoys it, it ceases to be a vested interest and becomes a hard-won reward. When a vested interest is enjoyed not by a minority but by a majority, it is a human right."

A rather hefty lady, aboard a crowded Fifth Avenue bus, trod upon the foot of an irritable merchant who was trying to read the stock tables in the evening paper. "Madam," he said coldly, "I will ask you kindly to get off my foot." "Put your foot where it belongs," she replied sharply. "Madam," he murmured reverently, "Don't tempt me!!"

AIR TRAVEL

A Campbell County woman, upon reaching her 100th birthday, was offered by her children a ride to Disney World by way of jet liner. "You won't get me in one of those fool contraptions," she assured firmly. "I'm gonna sit right here and watch my color TV like the good Lord intended I should."

We had another local lady who weighed around 300 pounds on a flight to L.A. A stewardess tapped her on the shoulder shortly after takeoff and invited her to move from the tourist section to the first class compartment. "I am flattered," said the lady, "but wonder why you've singled me out for this V.I.P. treatment?" "Madam," explained the stewardess cordially, "We have a weight-balance problem."

As the plane was about to depart from the gate, a man rushed up to the gate attendant and demanded, "Will there be time for me to get on the plane and kiss my wife goodbye?" The attendant answered, "That depends, sir, on how long you've been married."

OTHER TRAVEL

A doctor from our area applied for the job of ship's surgeon for a "round the world" cruise. "What would you do," he was asked, "if the captain fainted on the bridge?" "I would bring him to," answered the doctor. "And if he was still wobbly?" "I would bring him two more."

We had a local man to take a "round the world" cruise and come back with this report about Europe: He couldn't get hamburgers in Hamburg, English muffins in England, London broil in London, French toast in France, or even eggs Florentine in Florence. The wine and the girls, however were wonderful.

Louis Sobol tells a story about the American tourist motoring in Rome. He stopped a native and asked anxiously, "Do you have any black cats here two feet long?" "A few, signore," answered the native. "Any black cats four feet long?" It is possible, signore," conceded the native. "Well, have you any six feet long?" "But no, signore, that is ridiculous," said a native. "It's like I told you, you dope," interrupted the American's wife from the back seat, "you've run over a priest!"

There was a very large lady who threatened to file suit against the owner of a weighing machine in Japan while visiting there. She gave this account: "I stepped on the scale one morning and reached for the card that was supposed to register my correct weight. The card came out alright, but what it said was, 'Come back in fifteen minutes-alone'!!"

While in the country of Japan, a merchant made handy copies of local highway codes and regulations, (for American visitors) thoughtfully translated by himself into English.

A typical paragraph: "On Encountering Pedestrians: When a passenger on the hoof hooves into sight, tootle the horn, trumpet to him melodiously at first. If he still obstacles your passage, tootle him with increasing vigor and express by word of mouth the warning: Hi! Hi!"

OTHER INFO

A very astute Campbell County man drove all day in 95-degree temperature with every window of his car closed tight, then collapsed of prostration when he got home. "Why didn't you open the windows?" asked his wife. "What?" he protested weakly, "and let everybody know we haven't got an air-conditioned car?"

This can be found on an old tombstone in a private cemetery on "Poor House Road": "Here Lies Sam Billings. He Done His

Damndest."

Here are a few quotes I picked up along the way. Maybe they were original or maybe they weren't, I'm gonna tell them as I received them.

Will Rogers: "A husband who says he is boss in his own home is probably a liar about others things too."

Dicky Wills: "Mini skirts come in three sizes: short, shorter, and Good Morning, Judge."

Calvin Coolidge: "If you really want a job done, give it to a busy, important man. His secretary will do it."

Tommy Lasorda: On Paul Molitor: "He couldn't hit water if he fell out of the boat."

Jack Benny: "Give me my golf clubs, the fresh air, and a beautiful girl for a partner, and you can keep my golf clubs and the fresh air."

Groucho Marx: "A man is as old as the woman he feels."

Buddy Jennings: "A salesman should never be ashamed of his calling. He should be ashamed of his not calling."

William Wrigley, Jr.: "When two men in the same business agree, one of them is unnecessary."

J.A. Hopper: "If you lay down with dogs, you'll end up with fleas every time."

Sam Levenson: "My mother got up every morning at 5:00 a.m. no matter what time it was."

B.W.H, On especially looking for a publisher: "You'll find in life that the only helping hand is at the end of your own sleeve."

D.H.: "The hardest job in getting to the top of the ladder of success is getting thru the crowd at the bottom of the ladder."

Stan Vonn Grabil: "When opportunity knocks on the front door, most people are out in the backyard looking for a four-leaf clover."

Cicero: "More is lost by indecision than by wrong decision."

Andrew Carnegie: "Show me a man who can make a quick decision, stick to that decision, and act on that decision, and I'll show you a man who will make a fortune."

Jerry Falwell: "I give them humor and while their mouth is open I cram something in there they can chew on."

John F. Kennedy: "Success has a thousand fathers, failure is an orphan."

Carl Sandburg: "A baby is God's opinion that the world should go on."

W.S. Phelps: "The man who invented pills was a very bright fellow-but the man who put the sugar-coating on them was a genius."

Charles Brower: "A new idea is delicate. It can be killed by a sneer or a yawn. It can be stalled to death by a quip and worried to death by a frown on the right man's brow."

Alexis de Tocqueville: "We succeed in enterprises which demand the positive qualities we possess, but we excel in those which can also make use of our defects."

Will Rogers: "I never met a man I didn't like."

Jackie Gleason: "The second day of a diet is always easier than the first. By the second day you're off it."

Eddie Hamlett: "Every time I found a girl who could cook like my mama, she looked like my daddy."

B.W.H: "Bad officials are elected by good citizens who do not vote."

J.A.H, Upon turning 92: "Eighty is a wonderful age especially when you're seventy."

W.C. Fields: "If at first you don't succeed, try, try, a couple of times more, then quit. There's no sense in making a fool of yourself."

Jim Bibee: "A pitcher's success depends upon clean living and a fast friendly outfield.

Mark Twain: "Few of us can stand prosperity. Another man's, I mean.

Neil Morgan: "Behind every successful man is a surprised mother-in-law."

From a review of my book: "This is not a book that should be tossed aside lightly. It should be thrown with great force."

B.C. Forbes: "Without loyalty, nothing can be accomplished in any sphere. The person who renders loyal service in humble capacity will be chosen for higher responsibilities: Just as the biblical servant who multiplied the one pound given him by his master was made ruler over ten cities, where as the servant who did not put his pound to use lost that which he had."

Charles Baudelaire: "He that leaveth nothing to chance will do few things wrong, but will do very few things.

Charles F. Kettering: "You never stub your toe standing still. The faster you go, the more chance there is of stubbing your toe, but the more chances you have of getting somewhere."

Calvin Coolidge: "No person was ever honored for what he received. Honor has been the reward for what he gave."

Henry Clay: "Statistics are no substitutes for judgment."

Ed Moses: "Work as hard as you can, get as much as you can, give as much as you can."

Leon Bloy: "Love does not make you weak, because it is the source of all strength, but it makes you see the nothingness of the illusory strength on which you depended before you knew it."

Virginia Steele: "Nothing in life can compare with the thrill of knowing God and knowing He knows you."

Elbert Hubbard: "The man who has no more problems to solve is out of the game."

Samuel Smiles: "We learn wisdom from failure much more than from success. We often discover what will do by finding out what will not do, and probably he who never made a mistake never made a discovery."

Dore Schary: "If you have a weakness, make it work for you as a strength--and if you have a strength, don't abuse it into a weakness."

Jim Elliot: "The man is no fool who gives up what he cannot keep to gain what he cannot lose."

Oliver Wendell Holmes: "The great thing in the world is not so much where we stand as in what direction we are moving."

Tony Randall: "Those stretch pants so many young ladies are sporting these days come in three sizes: small, medium, and don't bend over."

Harry Mann: "The best way to make a fire with two sticks is to make sure one of them is a match."

Dave Gardner: "If it wasn't for Thomas Edison, we'd all be watching TV in the dark."

Jack Harmon: "A cat that jumps on a hot stove will never do it again. In fact, he won't even jump on a cold one."

Adiai Stevenson: "There is nothing more horrifying than stupidity in action."

Yogi Berra: "The game is never over till it's over."

Ike Eisenhower: "Business men should get into politics and fast."

Longinus: "In great attempts it is glorious even to fail."

A.E. Downing: "Great opportunities come to all, but many do not know they have met them. The only preparation to take advantage of them is simple fidelity to what each day brings."

Moncius: "The man of true greatness never loses his child's heart."

George Steinbrenner: "Show me a good loser and I'll show you a loser."

John Mason Brown: "Reasoning with a child is fine, if you can reach your child's reason without destroying your own."

O.O. McIntyre: "There are no illegitimate children. There are only illegitimate parents."

Senator Sam J. Ervin: "A young fellow with a cantankerous mother-in-law received a telegram from an undertaker. 'Your mother-in-law died today. Shall we cremate or bury?' The young man wires back: 'Take no chances. Cremate and bury'."

Senator Josh Lee: "A preacher who had been in the pulpit over an hour saw that the church's number one deacon had gone to sleep. So he told one of the ushers, 'Wake Brother Brown up.' The usher replied, 'Wake him up yourself, you put him to sleep'."

Congressman Tip O'Neill: "An eighty-five-year-old wanted to be a caddie--'Are your eyes good?' the golf pro asked. 'My eyes are perfect,' said the would be caddie. The pro said O.K. and assigned the senior citizen to a golfer. On the first hole, the golfer drove the ball 270 yards. 'Did you see where it went?' the golfer asked. 'I sure did,' the old man said, 'my eyes are perfect.' Then where did it go?' he asked. 'I forgot,' said the old man."

Congressman Brooks Hays: "A criminal lawyer was questioning his client, a recent widow. 'Did you hear your husband's last words?' he asked. 'Sure,' she answered. 'What were they?' 'Go ahead and shoot. You couldn't hit the broad side of a barn'."

Congressman Andrew Jacobs, Jr.: "A man was showing a friend his new house. 'This is the living room and this is the dining room,' the host explained. 'This is the den and this is my wife,' he added pointing to a woman clenched in a passionate embrace with another man. Having shown the house to his friend, the host invited him into the kitchen and poured each of them a cup of coffee. By now the guest could stand it no longer and asked, 'What about the guy in the den?' the host answered, 'Let him get his own coffee'."

Pablo Picasso: "There are two kinds of women--goddesses and doormats."

Benjamin Franklin: "Beware of little expenses: a small leak will sink a great ship."

Anonymous: "Wealth is not only what you have, but it is also what you are."

Anonymous: "Today's trying times will become tomorrow's good old days."

Anonymous: "Even a big man all wrapped up in himself makes a small package."

Anonymous: "What you don't know won't help you."

Anonymous: "He serves himself best who serves his customers best."

Anonymous: "That lucky rabbit's foot didn't work for the rabbit."

S.M.: "Friendship should be a responsibility, never an opportunity."

S.M.: "There is no right way to do a wrong thing."

S.M.: "Oversleeping will not make your dreams come true."

S.M.: "No age has a monopoly on success. Any age is the right age to start doing."

S.M.: "The person who wins may have been counted out several times, but didn't hear the referee."

Ken Crawford: "Stopping at third base adds nothing to the score."

SM: "It isn't what you know that counts, it's what you think of in time."

SM: "Life is a one way street, and you're not driving back."

TB: "Flattery is like perfume--to be smelled, not swallowed."

Tom Dreier tells about a Missouri school superintendent who chose this method to present "a picture of the world his students could understand:"

"If," said the superintendent, "the almost three billion persons in the world were compressed into a single town of 1,000 people, the following contrasts could be seen: 60 persons would represent the USA, the 940 all others. 60 Americans would receive half the income, 940, the other half.

303 would be white, the others non-white would be 697.

The 60 Americans would have a life expectancy of over 70, the others under 40.

The 60 Americans would consume 15 percent of the town's food supply, and the lowest income group of the Americans would be better off than the average of the 940.

The 60 Americans would have 12 times as much electricity, 22 times as much coal, 21 times as much oil, 50 times as much steel, and 50 times as much equipment as all 940 remaining members of the town.

Still feeling sorry for yourselves?"

An Old Fable--

"He who knows not, and knows not he knows not - he is a fool. Shun him.

He who knows not, and knows he knows not - he is simple. Teach him.

He who knows, and knows not he knows - his is asleep. Wake him.

But he who knows, and knows he knows. He is wise. Follow him."

We had a very well-to-do farmer in our community who was on his death bed. His family gathered about him, and simulated confidence in his recovery. "You're looking much better," his wife assured him. "The color is back in your cheeks," said his son. "You are breathing easier. Daddy," his daughter replied. The old farmer nodded and smiled weakly. "Thank you all," he whispered. "I'm going to die cured."

A traveling salesman came through our neighborhood years ago and stopped at our house following three or four days of heavy rains. Several roads had washed out a few bridges here and there. "This looks like the flood," he observed to myself and my sister. "The what?" my sister asked. He repeated, "The flood, you know the flood, when Noah saved the animals on the ark. You must have read about that." My sister assured him gravely, "Mister, on account of all this rain I ain't seen a paper in four or five days."

Old Proverb: "The feeling of health can only be gained through sickness."

P.M.: "No one's credit is as good as his money."

B.H.: "Nobody minds being interrupted, if it's by applause.

Proverb: "Never cut what you can untie."

G.W.T.: "A winner never quits and a quitter never wins."

B.W.H.: "If you want people to speak well of you, never speak well of yourself."

S.M.: "An ounce of hustling is worth a ton of rustling."

Walt Heuls: "What you think can't be done--somebody else is doing."

Warren Shaffer: "The salesperson who kills time eventually is killed by time."

S.M.: "Empty hands swell the easiest."

S.M.: "Nothing succeeds like courtesy and it doesn't cost a cent."

S.M.: "Nothing can stop people with the right attitudes from achieving their goals."

Ed Updyke: "When the elephants are restless in the valley the natives head for the mountains."

Bonnie Burnette's favorite definition is of an egotist: "A man who talks about himself, when you want to talk about yourself."

Shirley Hopper says, "Television permits you to be entertained in your living room by characters you wouldn't ordinarily allow in your living room."

Olivia Bagby says, "A 'Career Woman' is a woman who goes out and earns a 'man's' salary instead of staying home and taking his."

Betty O. McDaniel believes: "Sympathy is what you give a friend or relative when you don't want to lend them money."

Rodney Laughon lives by this very famous quotation: "Never, ever, give up."

Connie Martin believes: "Commitment is like the suicide squeeze in baseball, there is no going back."

Shawn McGuigan says: "People who are disappointed in love are compulsive eaters."

"The Little Old-Fashioned Lady"

There was a nice lady who was a little old-fashioned. She was planning a week's vacation in Florida at a particular campground, but she wanted to make sure of the accommodations.

Uppermost in her mind were toilet facilities, but she couldn't bring herself to write "toilet" in a letter. After considerable deliberation, she settled on "BC" standing for the words "bathroom commode."

Does the campground have its own "BC"? is what she actually wrote.

The campground owner was baffled by the euphemism, so he showed the letter around to several campers, but they could not decipher it either. Finally, the campground owner figured she must be referring to the location of the local Baptist Church, so he sat down and wrote:

Dear Madam,

I regret very much the delay in answering your letter, but I now take the pleasure in informing you that a BC is located nine miles north of the campground, and is capable of seating 250 people at one time. I admit, it is quite a distance away if you are in the habit of going regularly, but no doubt you will be pleased to know that a great number of people take their lunch along and make a day of it. They usually arrive early and stay late.

The last time my wife and I went was six years ago, it was so crowded we had to stand up the whole time we were there. It may interest you to know that right now there is a supper planned to raise money to buy more seats. They're going to hold it in the basement of the BC.

I would like to say that it pains me very much not to go more regularly, but it is surely no lack of desire on my part. As we grow older, it seems to be more of an effort, particularly in cold weather.

If you decide to come down to our campground, perhaps I could go with you for the first time, sit with you and introduce you to all the other folks. Remember, this is a friendly community.

THOUGHT FOR THE DAY

Nothing that comes from God is accidental!!!!

CONFIDENCE

A winner has confidence in the future. He has no doubt that the best is yet to come. In 1881 the College of William and Mary, in Virginia, closed its doors for seven years. It had survived devastation of the Civil War and had struggled to stay open during the bitter days of reconstruction, but finally it was forced to give up. Yet every morning during those seven barren years, when there were no students and the faculty was gone, President Ewell made it a point to ring the college bell. It was an act of faith. President Ewell believed that College of William and Mary would one day open its doors again and so he tolled the bell of confidence in the future.

During the bombings in London in World War II, a little girl prayed: "Oh God, take care of Daddy and Mommie and Billy and me, and please take good care of yourself, for if anything happens to you, we are all sunk." A winner has confidence in God who made him and who makes him a winner.

As Abe Lincoln's mother lay dying, she expressed her undying confidence in her son, as she said, "Abe, be somebody."

A young couple had been married only a month when the new bride covered the town opening charge accounts for herself at every store. The puzzled husband asked her, "Why was it necessary for you to have an account at every store in town?" "But, honey," she responded, "I want you to know that I have complete confidence in you."

"The uninhibited, yet brilliant architect, Frank Lloyd Wright, was once testifying in court. After identifying himself by name, the question was put to him: "What is your occupation?" He straightened up, adjusted the silk handkerchief in his suit pocket, and rapped his cane on the floor for emphasis, as he replied, "I'm the world's greatest living architect." When a shocked friend inquired how he could say such a thing, Wright answered simply, "I had to. I was under oath." How's that for confidence?

In the third game of the 1932 World Series, with the New York Yankees playing the Chicago Cubs, the indomitable Babe Ruth was at bat with two strikes against him. He stepped back from the plate and pointed out to right field. The ball was thrown and Ruth knocked it over the right field fence. He believed he could do it, and he did, because he believed in himself.

NEEDS

Everybody has needs. A man who had made a fortune built an enormous mansion with three swimming pools. One was filled with cool water, another with warm water, and a third was left empty. One day a guest questioned him about the empty pool, to which he replied, "Oh, you'd be surprised how many of my friends can't swim." It is not surprising that our needs vary.

A disturbed patient made regular visits to his psychiatrist for two years. Finally he was told that he was cured and ready to be dismissed. "Yeh, some cure!" scoffed the patient. "Two years ago, when I started coming to you, I was Gen. Robert E. Lee. Now that I'm cured, "I'm nobody." Everybody is set on being somebody.

We need faith, something to hold on to, and something that will hold us in hour of need. An atheist, rushing out of church one Sunday, was heard to exclaim: "Thank God I'm an atheist."

A preacher's son was asked one day why he believed in God. He replied, "Well, in my case, it just runs in the family."

A newspaper asked the question: "Who are the happiest people on earth?" The prize-winning answers were these: "A craftsman or artist whistling over a job well done. A little child building sand castles. A mother, after a busy day, bathing her baby. A doctor who has finished a difficult and dangerous operation, and saved a human life." These people went beyond themselves.

A man's love for children was questioned when he called a neighbor to complain about his five-year-old son. He had just paved his driveway and Tommy was marching back and forth in the fresh cement. "Don't you like children?" came the question from the neighbor. The perturbed man replied, "Yes, I like children in the abstract, but I can't stand them in the concrete!"

As two college professors were strolling across the campus one day, their conversation concerned the human body and the fact that it is 92 percent water. Just then a shapely young lady passed and their conversation was interrupted by "girl watching." Then said one of them to the other. "She's sure done a lot with her eight percent hasn't she?"

A brother of mine was so slow and shiftless at his job and the manager finally had no choice but to fire him. When someone found he had been fired he asked the manager if the vacancy had been filled, "No," said the manager, "he didn't leave a vacancy."

Claude Hopper had two quotations that had always inspired me after accumulating his first million dollars:

1. "All I've done in accumulation of material things has been an accident of ignorance."

2. "I always remember I can't out give God."

- " If Noah would have been smart, he would have swatted those two mosquitoes." - Helen Castle

- We have enough youth... How about fountain of smart?!

- A word to the wise is sufficient; but who can remember the word?

- The road to success is dotted with many tempting parking places.

- Employment applications always ask (or did in my day) who is to be notified in case of emergency? I always filled in "a very good doctor." It was great for the interview.

- A man went to his doctor whining - "Doc, I keep seeing spots before my eyes." "Why did you come to see me? Have you seen your ophthalmologist?" replied the doctor. "No," said the man. "Just these spots."

- My kid kept telling the teacher the dog ate his homework. Nobody believed him until his dog graduated from YALE!

- If you lead a horse to water; most people can... but if you can get him to float on his back, then you've really got something.

- Why don't seagulls fly over the bay? Because if they did they would be called bagels...

- Inside every older person, there's a young person yelling, "What happened?!"

- A comedian or "humor guy" like myself was described the other day as a man who has young ideas for old jokes.

- Did you hear about the man who sued for divorce because of a book? His wife read "Tale of Two Cities" - they had twins; then she read "The Three Musketeers" - they had triplets; He left when she brought home "Birth of a Nation"!!

- There is an old saying that brunettes have a sweeter disposition than blondes and red heads. However, I heard a man say his wife had been all three and he didn't see a difference.

- A member asked his pastor how he got the cut on his face - Pastor said he was shaving and thinking about the sermon and cut himself. The member says "next time, think about shaving and cut the sermon."

- A pastor was heard saying his church people would be first to go up in rapture... He gave his reason: "The Bible says, the dead in Christ shall rise first.

- The woman was asked ... "Whatever happened to that stupid ole blonde your husband used to run with?" She answered, "I dyed my hair".

- The doctor told me when he prescribed a new medicine to always take it after a hot bath... that was a little rough because I had a rough time drinking the hot bath...

- I'm gonna put all my money into taxes... It's definitely gonna go up.

- I went into a tax collector's office last week, sat down, smiled and a head clerk said, "May I help you, sir?" I said, "no, I just wanted to meet the people I work for."

- Daddy said to me as a teenager, "Be home by 11:00 or I'm locking the door." I said, "Is that a promise?

- When Dean Hopper was in school, he'd come home at report card time, hand it over to his parents and say, "I'm tired of TV anyway."

- I'll never forget as a teenager, Claude had a Chevy Belaire, Monroe had a Mercury Montere, and I had a Plymoth Fury. I told them, "Look, my car is in the Bible." They said, "Wayne, you ain't pullin' that on us." Momma chimed in and said, "Yeah Wayne, I ain't ever heard that." I said, "Yes. It's in the first book. It says right here - God drove Adam and Eve out of the garden in a fury."

THESE NEXT FEW CAN BE PERFORMED ANYWHERE

- The only reason I'm here is to show you that every 60 seconds, mental illness strikes...

- One out of every four people is mentally ill - Take a look to your left and right at the nearest four people. If they look okay, you're the one.

- I asked my wife if she likes mediums. I was trying to determine whether I should go to a mind reader or palmist. She said without hesitation, "You should go see a palmist - we're pretty sure you have a palm."

- Thirteen preachers were flying to a convention and they said to the stewardess - Tell the captain 13 preachers are praying for the planes safety - When she passed back by, they asked her what the pilot said. - "He said he'd rather have 4 engines working than 13 preachers praying."

- In the army they taught us to do war games without ammunition or weapons. In place of a rifle go "Bang, Bang", instead of a knife go "stab, stab", instead of grenade go "hole, hole". The war games started and a soldier went "bang, bang", nothing. He then ran up and went "stab, stab", nothing. "Hole, hole", nothing. Finally he went to the enemy and said, "I went bang-bang, stab-stab, and hole-hole and you didn't fall over dead." The enemy replied, "I'm a TANK."

- A Scottie's shoe repair shop ticket was found in Daddy's pocket when he passed. It was a pickup slip for shoes being repaired. The ticket was five years old - We went down and showed the ticket to Scottie who then took the ticket to the back. He came in from the back and said, "They'll be ready Wednesday."

- I went into the super market when I was in college and got a pint of milk, oranges and a Hershey bar. I put it on the counter and the clerk said, "I bet you're single." I said "How'd you know?" She replied, "Because you're ugly."

FUNNY CLAIM FORMS
FOLLOWING AUTO ACCIDENTS
(Taken from a Toronto newspaper)

- Coming home, I drove into the wrong house and collided with a tree I don't have.

- The other car collided with mine without giving warning of its intentions.

- I thought my window was down, but found it was up when I put my head through it.

- A pedestrian hit me and went under my car

- The guy was all over the road. I had to swerve a number of times before I hit him.

- In my attempt to kill a fly, I drove into a telephone pole. An invisible car came out of nowhere, struck my vehicle and vanished

- The telephone pole was approaching fast. I was attempting to swerve out of its path when it struck my front end.

Until Next Time:

In closing out the book, let me give you a few last
minute tips for speechmaking:

1. Tell as short of story as possible.

2. Don't laugh too much at your own material.

3. Don't tell "funny" stuff at the wrong time.

4. Don't use "funny" stuff at the wrong engagement.

5. Don't repeat a "funny" story at the request of anyone at an
engagement.

6. Don't use material unknown to your audience.

Your Notes:

Your Notes: